The Dream Speaks Back

Leslie Tate, Sue Hampton & Cy Henty

TSL Publications

First published in Great Britain in 2019
By TSL Publications, Rickmansworth
Copyright © 2019 Leslie Tate, Cy Henty, Sue Hampton

ISBN / 978-1-912416-98-1

The right of Leslie Tate, Cy Henty & Sue Hampton to be identified as the author of this work has been asserted by the author in accordance with the UK Copyright, Designs and Patents Act 1988.

All characters and events in this publication, other than those clearly in the public domain, are fictitious and any resemblance to actual persons, living or dead, is purely coincidental.

All rights reserved. No part of this publication may be reproduced, stored in a retrieval system or transmitted, in any form or by any means without the prior written permission of the publisher, nor be otherwise circulated in any form of binding or cover other than that in which it is published and without a similar condition being imposed on the subsequent buyer.

Front Cover: So what are we going to do now Daniel? – painting by Cy Henty.
Concept a collaboration between Cy Henty and Daniel Maher.
Back Cover: Sue Hampton, Leslie Tate and Cy Henty, photographed by Katherine Paley.
For other photos and copyright holders, see end of book

DEDICATION

Cy Henty: for Dylan, Dad and Dan.
Sue Hampton: for Paul.
Leslie Tate: for Rosemary and Robert.

LIFTING THE STONE

—— *Leslie* ——

I woke up this morning in a short, soft bed, tucked behind the door of a room the size of a train compartment. In my mind it was half-dark, so I could see the cupboard at the bottom of the bed and the planes and rockets on the wallpaper. Outside I could hear birdsong and the chink-chink of a milk float; inside was quiet. My eyes travelled the room, exploring the long wooden box beneath the window and the thick-lined curtains. The box had a red-cushioned seat which became, as I watched it, a low chest of drawers where my mum on washing days would stow away my socks and undies. That's in the top two drawers, both with plastic handles, while the wide drawer beneath has everything I need for my imaginary journey. It's as if there's a weight pressing down on the box; it's bowed in the middle like a worn sofa, and the big bottom drawer often jams.

The room is a capsule on a launch pad and I'm counting down, but only because I know it's too early to get up. As I count I imagine my dad's voice telling me to stay where I am. He's the Deadwood Sheriff behind the door and he's got me covered. If I'm at the window when he bursts in, he'll shout, "Get yourself back to bed!"

The room opens out into a house, a three-bedroom semi, with floral wallpaper and matching curtains. Inside is empty and unreal. The exact size is hard to make out. Look up, it's a cathedral; down, and it's a doll's house; close your eyes and it's a dungeon. There's a faint, reflective glow all around, like water in a bowl. Outside, the walls are castle-thick, with concrete front steps, pebble-dashed bays and black-painted drainpipes; inside, it's a stop-over camp where no one can see me. The words of my mum echo in my ears: *If you make your bed you can lie in it.* I'm the stowaway child in a silent house; I'm steering the ship.

When it's time to get up my mum is there, setting out the table. She's a short, busy woman with peery eyes whose hands move quickly. "Eat up," she says briskly. My dad's there, too, chewing toast. His face is thin and bristly and his mouth moves up and down, slowly. I can't tell what he's thinking. Sitting opposite me, I think he's on guard, maybe to defend me but maybe as a warning. The word he uses for being like this is *ruminating*. He's a large grazing animal preparing for the day.

In my mum's world it's all about tasks. She wants us to get through breakfast before anything can go wrong. She's hard at it, worrying about the day ahead. Once she's taken me to school the place will be hers. I know, because she's said so, as we walk. When she talks like that she speaks out loud in a matter-of-fact way, as if I wasn't there. Of course I'm also being talked to, as her friend. I like it when she does that because it brings us together. Sometimes she's the singsong lady on the phone, and at other times she's silent. That's when I feel the struggle inside her and begin to worry. It's as if there's a pipe leaking in the bathroom, filling up the house. The weight of water slows things down; it blocks up the windows and the doors. Inside, we're running out of air and space. The house is a black box with the lid jammed down. It takes an effort not to cry.

Today is an *are-you-ill?* day. I'm being asked if I feel all right. It's said like a challenge, for my own good. When I don't answer, my face is looked at and further questions are asked. I'm being given a chance to change my story; but I'm aware that if I'm really sick it won't end there. I'll be asked about what I did to make myself poorly. It'll also be on my record. So I'm in the spotlight, and my best chance is to agree while saying as little as possible. I've a secret hope that my illness might be enough to keep me off school.

We eat in the front room. It's back to breakfast, as if the illness questions never happened. Did I imagine it? Or was I acting as some sort of mind reader? Could I sense my mum's thoughts, hearing the words *off colour* and *peaky* at a distance, like talk from another room? Or were they all part of my story, a dream of being cared-for because I was special? Whatever she'd said, her words carried weight. They seemed more real than my thoughts or the food on the table. Even in silence I could hear her words. They sounded like rain on glass.

We're finishing off breakfast and my mother's eyes are on the clock. It's a school day, and I'm already thinking about the journey and waving goodbye at the gates. I hear children singing and see my wild boy self, running in the yard. The wind is up and my words come in snatches. Suddenly I've lost my footing and I'm falling. It happens in a breath and I'm sprawling, looking up at the sky, feeling nothing. It's a nice place to be, like playing all day on a beach. Someone leans down and asks me if I'm OK and for a moment I'm tucked up in bed. When the pain begins it's all down my arm. My skin feels swollen, as if it's been too close to an electric fire. The wound is gritty and when I'm taken to the nurse she tut-tuts and scrubs it with a flannel. If I wriggle, her fingers grip hard, and if I cry out she tells me to act like a man. Afterwards, my arm aches then goes limp. As I rise from the chair I can feel it hanging like a broken branch. I hold it out of sight so my mum and dad don't suspect anything.

I'm in bed again, propped up on pillows. On the cupboard by the bed there's a clock, a hankie and a glass of water. My pyjamas smell of *Vicks* and my head's full of cold. The taste of medicine is still in my mouth. The door's wide open, so I can hear my mum as she's coming upstairs. Putting on my sad face, I get ready for her visit. I'm stuck in my room, only allowed out to use the toilet.

"School tomorrow for you," she says in her no-nonsense voice. I can hear my grandma in it, adding the word *lad* at the end.

After she leaves, the room changes to a hospital: an isolation ward. I'm between ice-white sheets in a bed of my own. My condition is serious but I'm bearing it bravely. Secretly, I enjoy being ill; it relieves me of responsibility and softens what people say. As I lie looking at the ceiling, it seems possible that I might be unwell for a very long time. I've aged, turning into a pair of eyes staring out of a tired face. I can picture myself leaving the ward, leaning on a stick with my parents at my side. Their voices are hushed and they walk at my pace, which is slow and deliberate, like a funeral procession. The funeral is mine, of course, or will be mine if they're not careful. I've a light in my head and a swelling inside that no one can see. At any time I might blow up and fill the room as the Red Balloon Boy and float off through the window.

When they find I've gone I'll be watching through a camera from above. I'll scare them with voices that come from the cupboard. When my dad pulls it open I'll switch to the chest of drawers, then to the light bulb, then beneath the bed. I watch him search the room while my mum backs off, calling my name. After they've left I hear them downstairs speaking in whispers. My mum's voice is shaky; my dad's comes in bursts. Some of the words I hear are *worried, mystified, baffled*. They sound strangely familiar but not-quite-right, like a TV impersonator or long-distance caller speaking on the phone.

When I hear my dad phoning the police, I realise suddenly what I've done. I want to run downstairs and ask him to stop: I'm OK, I'll plead, it was all just a joke. But I can't. There's a weight on me of fear or guilt for who I am; I've fallen in the playground and they're coming to get me. In any case I'm too ill – really sick, weighed down with illness, tingling all over and beginning to sweat – and the fantasy has stopped. I've run home from school and sneaked in the back door, with questions to answer. I try an excuse but no one believes me and I get told off. Now that's over I've brushed my teeth and I'm in bed. As I count down, my breath comes slowly and sleep is near. When I wake I'll be myself, waiting to get up ...

I'm just a boy waking in the morning in a short, soft bed in a room the size of a train compartment, making my way to heaven.

Sue

The little girl liked the things inside, where she couldn't see them. Not with her eyes. Feelings were so deep in there that no one else felt them, except Daddy – if they were looking at the same tree or bud and holding hands. Stories were magic like that, because the feelings weren't really on the page but catching anyway. They burst out of the book and when the story ended they were still part of her. And somehow, inside they were hers. Even if a million zillion children had read *The Snow Queen* and *The Lord of the Rushie River*, Gerda and Susan were her best friends, and the sadness was a kind of secret between them.

The girl was a child who cried because stories made her, and if they didn't she might not read them again. Sometimes living on the outside felt very hard, and made her cheeks hot and her voice papery. The inside was a safer world where imagining made things real. Her outside was a lump. She'd heard a big boy say so in the street even though Mummy tried to talk over him and make her face bright. And her hair was wild and rough, not pretty. The pictures in stories were never like her but that didn't matter because inside she was brave and kind like *The Ugly Duckling* with feathers all stubby and brown. One day she might squidge out of her skin and fly, like the Red Admiral that landed just by Daddy's foot. He believed in fairies.

Daddy loved the garden because it never hurt anyone. So the little girl loved it too. He bought a small stone lion like Aslan, and every day she went to see him by the hedge. Leonard was always the same but always new. If he'd had adventures in the night, like Sparkle the lion troll from Hamleys, who flew around her bed because he was a prince in another land, he was always back by morning. He didn't smile because he knew about sadness. Lions did, especially if they were really Jesus.

There was a plum tree near Leonard but she was scared of the wasps. She was afraid of biting into the soft and shiny red skin, because some things that hid inside were scary. Like trolls under bridges but they didn't stop with THE END. Neither did the world under the top step in the back garden, the bit that sloped down to the railway in a wall of flowers.

"Can I see?" she asked, every summer.

"Are you sure?"

Daddy understood that she needed to look, even though she wished she hadn't. The stone slab was much too heavy for her to disturb but Daddy had laid it. As he lifted it, she crouched on her haunches to be close. Not that she would ever touch. Underneath the smooth grey lid with the broken edges, everything squirmed and slid and crawled and scampered and it was scratchy and dirty. It had its own smell like grass cuttings turning brown and slimy. The beetles looked hard but she could imagine the feel of their legs, scraping softly as if they were hardly there. It made her scalp itch under her dry curls. Worms looked chewy and bendier than fingers. She'd seen a thrush once, eating one, but white of egg was slippery enough to make her gag. "Just one mouthful," Mummy said, but she'd never get used to it. Her insides didn't want it and heaved. But it was the snakes under the paving stone that she had to see. They were the magic. They were the Daleks and the ogre. They didn't hiss or shoot forked tongues. They didn't curl out of baskets and dance to music. But they were quick and green enough to wrap around her like ribbon. Except that they didn't seem to care about her. Maybe they were blinded when Daddy stole the roof away. They were the kings of the soft brown darkness and their secret kingdom was just as they wanted it to be. That was why Daddy soon put the stone back again, so nothing underneath it was frightened.

The girl was frightened. The fear tickled but not in a giggly way. Her Clarks shoes with a bar and buckle were big enough to squash the snakes but she never would. Blood and bones were gaggier than egg white and imagining the softest sound underfoot was worse. Daddy said the creeping things were beautiful too but the girl didn't have his grown-up eyes or his grown-up brain. The snakes that pretended to be grass swarmed when she closed her eyes. They wound their way into her hair until she was a witch.

She didn't tell Daddy, though, or he wouldn't lift the stone again.

―― *Cy* ――

Leslie: What do you think about the idea that general creativity comes out of retaining one's childishness?

Cy: In a world where we are actively encouraged to systematically destroy our imaginative, playful, emotional, irrational, spiritual, surreal and artistic sides from a young age I believe, to an extent, that we become split in two. I'm not sure if it is retaining one's *childishness* as much as retaining one's fascination with the wonder and absurdity of life. Those who fight to retain these aspects of themselves are often beautiful and fragile people, while at the same time pushing society forward by being inspired or by perceiving the universe in a different way. They fight hard to retain their honesty and dignity in a world where people are expected to hide their true selves and toe the line. When my first comedy partner Sam Ball and I used to improvise in a warehouse many years ago, we would think of it as therapy in a way, but it was also *play*; and it is the ability to play that is lost. We would take on different characters, surprising each other, trying to outwit each other – but also often exploring many dark paths within ourselves and being quite brutal toward each other. Sometimes this led to hilarious results ... occasionally we'd go too far and that material was rarely put on stage! Always we would share a drink afterwards and feel relaxed and happy. The *play therapy* had not only given us some great material but exorcised a lot of our fears as we tried to make sense of an often cruel and incomprehensible world.

My second comedy partner Al Ronald and I also play in the same way, and challenge each other. The philosophy of our partnership is to remind our audience of the dynamic, beautiful yet chaotic position we are truly in. On a rock, spinning around a huge radioactive fireball in a

void. I try to remember this every morning. Is it worth worrying about the trivial? A lot of the constructs of society, it seems, are a dark theatre meant to distract us from our true reality – to direct us toward consumerism – and often toward a slavery of the mind. That instinctive and dynamic half of ourselves is chained up somewhere in the labyrinth beneath the domed ceiling of our skulls, and our mind's eye is blinded.

Leslie: I'm reminded of Baudelaire's, "Genius is nothing more nor less than childhood recaptured at will."

Cy: Yes I certainly agree with Baudelaire. I don't think it is immature to keep the artistic aspect of oneself alive, it is just that that part of us is often left behind in childhood because we are told to deny it, so that we will follow the often absurd rules of a selfish, mean-minded society. Truly, I believe human nature is loving and compassionate and that we are all imaginative and beautiful, and that if we can prise open the lids of our own mind's eyes – or help even for a moment others to do so, through games, through comedy, film, art and performance, through being honest to ourselves, through being able to laugh at ourselves – if we can cut through the bullshit pumped at us daily by the media moguls and corporations, we will rediscover the will to live wonderfully in what is often a surreal and absurd reality full of chaos, both terrifying and awe-inspiring.

My love of acting, writing, performance and visual art is because it allows that part of me to be free – and I hope connect with that part in others – that spark, that incredible light that we often catch a glimpse of behind the windows of the soul. It is never truly extinguished and we need to fan the flames in order to ignite it once more.

INSIDE STORIES

—— *Sue* ——

Daddy wasn't always home when the little girl went to bed but when his train was an early one they met him from the station, even if it was dark. There were so many men with raincoats and brown briefcases and polished shoes, but Daddy was different on the inside, and they were the only ones who knew. At bedtime, Mummy played the same tune on the piano so they could march around the living room twice, and once more for luck, and then along the hall to their twin beds. But if Daddy was home, when they'd cleaned their teeth and were tucked up in their jimjams, playtime was about to begin.

Sometimes, when her brother was only small, Mummy read a *Thomas the Tank Engine* story. The same one. The one where Mrs Kindly waved her red dressing gown and shouted, "Help!" as loudly as she could. Then Daddy would charge all the way from his armchair to the rescue. As if he thought there was a monster or a fire and there was no time to lose. His eyes would be wide open and he'd crash in like a train off the rails. The little girl and her brother would laugh so much they couldn't sit up straight for ages.

"It's just a story," Mummy would explain, and Daddy would sag with relief and go back to the living room.

Then Mummy knew what she had to do. Instead of turning the page she read the same one all over again, and again, until Daddy was too tired to run any more.

But there was another kind of bedtime when Daddy was home, and it was even better, but not as wild. It was the kind that couldn't always happen, if Daddy's day had been long or bad. The little girl knew when not to ask, because she saw in his eyes that he was all used up, and it made her want to hug him very gently. But when it was the right kind of bedtime, he told a story of his own. No one else's. He told a story that had never been heard before, because it wasn't born. Not until he began it. And then it grew. It was always funny and magical, because Daddy knew exactly what stories needed.

That was how the girl knew stories were inside as well as out. All she had to do was open her mouth and away they flew. So she was a teacher and the dolls and teddies were her class. Sometimes they had to write small, in little books she cut and folded for them, and Twinkle Troll couldn't spell but the little girl loved her best so she wrote in red, "Well tried". But what they all liked most was sitting on her lap for a story, or piling onto her bed when they knew she was meant to be asleep too so she had to whisper, and put a finger to her lips if anyone was jumpy with excitement. The stories were only for them and their tiny, fluffy or rubbery ears. So the words never needed to be crossed out and they never sounded silly.

If she remembered them next morning, she would write them down with pictures. If she was with Nana and Pop at the smart house, they could be in the story. So could the china ladies on the mantelpiece.

"I've written another book," she'd say. That always made Daddy happy.

This is her book.

Leslie

I met Cy Henty ten times before I met him.

The first time, we were playing with my dad making goony noises on the beach. Cy was Bloodknock, I was Bluebottle – and we dug for treasure, built dams to stop the tide and waved our arms at seagulls to scare 'em. Later, with the wind in our faces, we drew stick people with our fingers in the sand. We named them Yuri, Neil and Buzz.

Back in the house, Cy was the ghost boy beside me on the stairs. Like me, he could hear heavy breathing. Noises made him jump. He was there behind curtains, in the voice on the landing and the face at the window, the light left on and the rattle in the pipes. No one else could see him.

Once a year, we both ran riot at our birthday party, shouting out of windows and bouncing on beds.

"I'm flying!" cried Cy.

"I'm Leslie!" I replied.

"So who am I?" asked Cy, pulling funny faces.

"I'm tall!" I cried, standing on a chair.

Our daredevil climbs and downhill races had us sent out to the garden, where I dived to the ground and scraped both knees. We both went white and shaky, crying a lot. Later in the night Cy told me about story time with his sister. When he fell asleep I sneaked into my parents' bedroom and played at dressing up.

Cy was there in my dream, tracking strange beasts and roaming the woods while I stood guard by the fence. When the moon came up he danced with his uncle The Soupmaker. We were the forest kings – Moomin-Gruffalos who sang our songs. Our voices in darkness were heard by other children who came to join us, bringing their blankets and cuddly toys.

Cy, on lead vocals, sang, "Oh, wild thing."

I was on backup, echoing his song.

"You make my heart sing."

His voice was telling everyone to come out and play. When the children heard it they ran across and lined up behind him.

"Wild thing," Cy sang again, and I saw him lead the children, snaking around trees and jumping over ditches.

"You make everything ..." he cried, reaching a clearing where he pointed to some logs and the children all sat down.

"Grooooovy," he called, extending his arms.

When the song began again I was pen in hand, writing a poem. The words were small birds peering through the leaves. Cy was in sunlight, standing tall. His body was a flower with his head split open like an anatomical drawing. Suddenly the children had all turned to saplings.

—— *Cy* ——

Leslie: What were the signs during childhood that you might end up in the expressive arts?

Cy: When I was a boy my sister used to dress me up and we would act out improvised sketches. My mum and dad were always anarchic and playful, they encouraged our imaginations, but most of all our sense of humour. *Monty Python* was a coming-of-age, as was *Blazing Saddles* – both came from my dad. On the other side we had Mum reading us *Edward Lear* and Spike Milligan's *Milligananimals.* I was extremely lucky to have such imaginative parents. Life is never rosy, and living on the edge and appreciating the absurdity of life doesn't make it easy to exist in the accepted form of reality. Mum and Dad were passionate and irrational creatures at times. But they came honestly to the world and faced each other on that battlefield, I believe. To me, now, looking back I couldn't imagine being raised by anyone else. I wouldn't be me without the madness, water fights, fir cone fights, explorations into uncharted territory, fear, love, art, jazz music, dancing and paganism!

―― *Leslie* ――

Then I became Leslie. The change happened as a story, coming into my head as I did things. I was introduced to myself in the mirror and out there in the world, as boy, third-person.
"Who are you?" the boy in the mirror asked.
I didn't hear my answer.
"What's your name?"
As he said it, the room went silent.
"What can you do?"
I felt my other-self blushing.
"Can you kick a ball?"
I couldn't answer that.
"Do you have an army?"
That's Cy, my other-boy thought. That's Cy.

―― *Cy* ――

Leslie: Can you tell me how your interest in horror films and horror-comedy first began?
Cy: It stems from boyhood when I read Edgar Allan Poe's *Tales of Mystery & Imagination* and listened to them on a set of story-tapes read by Christopher Lee in his wonderful rich, deep, sonorous voice. During my youth, I enjoyed the high-camp and bright red blood of Hammer Horror, and early black-and-white sci-fi such as *The Day the Earth Stood Still*. I always liked the baddies as a child – I wanted to be Darth Vader in the playground – and Christopher Lee's Dracula, of course. I really think that as a sensitive and compassionate, gangly, accident-prone and awkward boy with a silver tooth, thick NHS glasses and a bowl-haircut, who was great at drawing but awful at sport, the lure of the *dark side* or bad guys

in fiction was precisely because they represented something so completely different from me. If I had known as a teenage boy that I would go on to act in independent horror films I would have grinned widely at the prospect!

—— *Leslie* ——

At school, Cy and Leslie sat at the same table and drew animals on textured foolscap. When they'd finished, they traced each other's hands, then pulled off their shoes to draw around their feet. On the way to the next lesson Cy stopped to say hello to the girls while Leslie walked on, writing poetry in his head. In the drama class afterwards Cy took the lead, playing *Leslie the Boy who lost his Tongue*. The show went out live on TV; it began with a guessing game.

"I'm *inside* the body. Sometimes outside," Cy called to the class.

"Pink," he replied when asked about the colour.

"No hairs," was his next answer.

"No bones," he said when asked for another clue.

"Muscles? I think so," he added, and went on answering until someone got it.

For the second half of the show Cy chased a tongue-shaped mitten held up by Leslie in a slow-mo dance. The pursuit went all over and was accompanied by Cy whinnying and revving up his motorbike. It ended with Leslie pulling off the mitten and throwing it high in the air. All heads turned as the mitten went up and hung there for a moment before it sprouted wings and flew off.

—— Cy ——

Leslie: Can you tell us about the other arm of your career – your work as a comedian?

Cy: I always loved playing characters on stage, although NEVER as myself – that's always scared me. So at infant school I wrote comedy plays for puppets, performing them with my friend in front of the whole school. Roll forward to secondary school and I was in a comedy band playing in assemblies with my talented Goth friend who struggled to fit my poetry to music! But for me it wasn't about the performance – more about creating a whole world. We had backstories for the characters and worked on album covers as well. At this point I was already writing reams of prose and poetry that I illustrated, filling up exercise books I'm guessing I got from my mum, who was a teacher. Performing was always the last step – and the most dangerous – although I think performing your own material is much scarier than performing other people's.

Leslie: I think you've been in a lot of comedy double acts. Can you tell us about them?

Cy: After my school double acts, I wrote surreal pieces for the university magazine and made short films with my friend Neil. My friendship with Sam Ball also began at university. Sam and I were lucky enough to perform alongside some of the greats on the comedy circuit in the nineties and tour universities with Russell Brand before playing at The Pleasance Theatre in the Edinburgh Festival with our show *Unhinged*. For the last 15 years I've been in another double act, *The Electric Head*, with my comedy partner Al Ronald.

Leslie: So why double acts?

Cy: I love working with someone – I'm a social creature! But perhaps it has to do with self-confidence too. With

Sam Ball and Al Ronald it was possibly to do with the fact that my mind can be quite manic and surreal and I often find it hard to shape or edit things into a language that others understand. The creative process for me can be an all-consuming, obsessive one and there is often a stream of consciousness that I have described as akin to having a biro stuck into my brain, with the thoughts flowing out onto the page like ink ... If you can share ideas and have someone you trust tell you the truth – "That bit doesn't make any sense Cy, how about this?" – it becomes a less fearful process.

—— *Leslie* ——

When Cy and Leslie grew up they wanted to write a book. They'd write it together, becoming their own characters – Cy the Actor and Chalk-Face Leslie. They told true stories, said it with their hands, and painted it on walls that only they could see. Their book would be a hold-all, an imaginary wardrobe full of feather masks and keepsakes and beads in a row. When they reached inside they'd come out with board games and clothes to fit giants. There were cracks at the back where snakes and spiders slept and a secret compartment filled with tear-stained hankies and dead wasps. At the bottom, underneath the coats, they found a map of their travels with photos to prove it, a box of magic tricks, and a *best of* collection of jokes, memories, reflections and open-ended stories.

This is their book.

—— *Sue* ——

Mummy had jobs to do but she made them into games they could play, like popping peas from a basket to a pan. She danced around the kitchen with a duster under her foot until the tiles smelt of lavender polish, and shone. In the kitchen she let the girl turn the handle to squeeze the water out of the clothes and press them flat. It was called a mangle but it was hard to work. Her little brother could move it because he was growing muscles. The girl didn't want any. Just to point her toes like Lorna Drake, ballet dancer in *Bunty*.

Her brother was smaller than her and funnier, with a nicer face and fairer, softer curls. She didn't know how to be naughty and she couldn't run like the wind. The girl was Little John. He was Robin. When Daddy hammered grips into the big tree with the wide, Sherwood trunk, her brother had climbed halfway up before she'd begun. She wanted to be like Mummy who played cricket and jumped out of windows and once landed in the Headmistress's flower bed but was let off because she was good as well as daring. But the little girl didn't know how it would feel, up high. She'd rather hide behind the trunk and pretend she  was safe inside it, like Robin when the Sheriff's men came. She'd rather tell her dolls a story about the squirrels that lived up there, ate acorns for tea and drank rain out of their little green cups.

"Come on!" cried her brother. He was smiling and his eyes were laughing again.

"Not too far up, Monkey!" said Daddy.

The girl watched. Inside things started to feel heavy the way they did when she didn't know the answer in Arithmetic. Or couldn't thread the needle even when it was soggy with lick, and pointy as a whisker. Or smelt the cabbage in the pan.

She reached for the first ring. All she had to do was pull the rest of her up, but she was a lump. Her brother wasn't. He was all bounce and spring. Daddy helped her. He told her she was all right and all she had to do was keep going.

"Don't look down."

As she reached for the next rung, he said she was getting the hang of it. But she felt as if she was hanging herself, and could drop and break like Humpty Dumpty or a baby bird that was scrawny, bony skin inside the shell. Her brother was sitting down, way above her, his legs swinging free. He was the king of the castle but what was she?

Maid Marian didn't climb because of her long dress. In the film she was like a nun, but beautiful as Nana's china ornaments shiny with paint. She didn't have frizzy hair and she wasn't too heavy for dancing.

The girl could reach the next grip but her body was stiff now as it stretched. The bark had scraped her knee and it burned.

"She's stuck!" said her brother.

And she was. Until Daddy saved her and told her not to worry, she could try again, and in any case trees were mostly for loving and breathing.

But she knew she was a story now, and it wasn't as funny as it would sound, even if she told it herself.

DREAM YOUR LIFE WITH GREAT CARE

—— *Cy* ——

Leslie: We all need a day job. Can you tell us about yours?

Cy: My first *proper job* after university was working with Sam Ball as an Occupational Therapy Assistant in a huge, old Victorian psychiatric hospital in Brentwood, Essex. It was an imposing redbrick asylum on a hill and I was thrown into a department attached to an assessment ward that I basically ran on my own. It opened my eyes, not only to the stigma surrounding mental health and the ignorance of others, but also to the pain and suffering of those dealing with its symptoms.

At the assessment ward I had a group, sometimes of up to ten or more patients, with a variety of diagnoses from schizophrenia to bipolar to alcohol-induced psychosis, as well as depression caused by bereavement and dementia. I would go around the ward in the morning and gather my group then ditch the official activities, which seemed to have been written on some yellowing timetable from the 1950s and included listening to Max Bygraves and Bingo. Someone had forgotten that these were intelligent human beings! We made up our own games. One particular session at a tea-break became a murder mystery investigation measuring the trajectory of an invisible bullet. We imagined that the heads of the hospital were trying to get rid of me for veering off the timetable and allowing the patients to have too much fun. Of course there were tragedies too and a lot of pain. Eventually when a patient killed himself I had to leave.

I ended up drinking too heavily and working in an administrative job for a branch of British Gas. However, in those days they used a number of fax machines to receive jobs from other departments and it became my task to monitor and file these; at the same time I had begun writing about my experiences at the hospital. It was a very lonely job as I was set apart from the rest of the office and in an attempt to reach out I decided to create a secret identity for myself as *The Faxman* and subversively fax poetry and artwork in this guise to the other offices up and down the country.

After two years I finally got back in contact with my comedy partner Sam Ball. Luckily a mutual friend, and a great actor, Paul Battin, who had directed our double act right from university, arranged a meeting. So once a week after work we would improvise in Sam's dad's warehouse, and on the train I would begin jotting down material. Unfortunately at the same time my first wife, whom I'd met at 26, suffered from terrible postnatal depression after giving birth to our son. To keep my dream alive, I got up early in the morning, looked after my son and his mum during the day and then sat at the typewriter all night writing comedy scripts.

Leslie: So how did you get back into the comedy circuit?

Cy: Eventually after a string of successful shows Sam Ball and I got an agent in London who at the time also handled Craig Charles of *Red Dwarf*, Russell Brand, Karl Theobold and Omid Djallili. Finally it seemed my dream was coming true and I would also be able to support my wife and son doing something that I loved ...

—— *Leslie* ——

During my working life I nearly gave up trying to write. Job survival was more important. As a secondary teacher, I had to focus on keeping going and delivering lessons. Later, as a manager in Further Education, I had to accept that no job was ever fully completed. With so many aspirational projects raining down from above, it was a question of *talk that talk* and get on with it. So each day was a dash, starting early, ending late, and *doing*, not thinking, was the watchword.

Work did have its compensations. It was sociable. The students offered a window on the world. There was a rhythm to the job, an immediate sense of being and doing and living in the present. It took skill and panache to juggle everything and stay on top – and even when I was worn out and frazzled, the seemingly-impossible task might still come off. So, telling myself this wasn't forever, I put my other life into a glass box.

At the weekend I'd usually manage a few unfinished pieces. They were my attempts to stay ahead. Proof to myself that I still could be an author, even though I knew my style was often imitative or too grand for the subject matter. But my writing habit, practised on Sundays, kept me in the frame. In the game against the world I was still in credit.

But to switch from a day job to writing isn't easy. The list mentality required by work doesn't sit well with holistic thought – and analysing performance and ticking boxes is a narrowing process. When you're busy-busy with a head full of competing priorities, it's hard to maintain a state of playful awareness.

Books don't write themselves. In my case, the long awaited inspirational moment never came. I was always preparing to write while *clearing the boards* for the week ahead. But really I was playing for time. To be busy getting ready was a handy excuse; it kept me in the zone while not putting anything to the test.

It was only when I stepped down as a manager that the real writing began. I learned about words – how they have to be listened to and tried all ways; their moods and their colours, and how they shape the narrative. Combined with character, they make the story.

I still work hard with words – or they work me – listening, positioning, pushing them together to see if they fit. And I write as a task, something I do every day, as a schedule, with effort.

So when I'm writing these words, everything else takes second place.

It's my job.

Sue

The little girl once sat on a horse. No sooner was she in the saddle than she asked to climb down. So she would never be a heroine. In her stories there were horses that didn't leave dollops to stink in the sun, or bare fierce teeth, or kick. They were loyal and gentle and galloped so fast they could outrun rivers and witches.

Sometimes she wrote about baddies who robbed banks but magic was safer. She wrote about treasure and spells, islands and castles, Robin Hood, mermaids and fairies. Once she'd met the March sisters in *Little Women*, she wanted to be Jo, but that was Mummy, really. Not her. When Mummy read the books to her, Beth got better, and her sisters

and Marmee and Hannah all cried with joy and said thanks to God. So when the little girl took the heavy books with their colour pictures to read under the covers, she found that Mummy had cheated. She wept, muffled, on her pillow. Why would Mummy pretend when she trusted her? It was hard to believe. And the happiness was a lie. But the sadness was much more beautiful. It didn't hurt like the fire when Amy burnt Jo's book.

Apart from stories, the girl wrote lists. Favourite books. Favourite characters. Favourite people (real), with Daddy at number one.

—— *Cy* ——

Leslie: Can you tell us what happened when *Sam and Cy* your comedy double act, got taken up by a London agent and *went big*?

Cy: We were fortunate enough, through this agent, to end up on The University Tour with Russell Brand. I remember him stripping off at one show and demanding a bottle of Jack Daniels from behind the bar, at another spraying the audience with a fire extinguisher and all of us getting escorted out by security. Sam and I had quite tightly scripted material but Russell had an absolute desire to be free, honest and throw off disguise. I found him intensely charming, warm and very loyal to the other comics on the bill; he was acutely intelligent and had a great energy about him. He invited Sam and me to see his first solo show in Edinburgh after he had been through rehab, and I'd never seen him so nervous. It was a great show – self-analytical and self-deprecating. Russell essentially bares his soul on stage and encourages his audience to shed their masks along with him.

At the same time Sam Ball and I had a run at The Canal Café Theatre, Camden, London, where we began to develop our own Edinburgh Festival show. Eventually we were given a slot at The Pleasance Theatre. For us, Edinburgh was an incredible experience – performing our show every day for a month meant that we knew the material inside out. In fact during one show where an audience member decided to walk out across the stage during our psychiatrist sketch, we actually swapped roles and did the rest of the show as each other.

The city is so exciting during the Festival that I never wanted it to end. In my real life I was going through a difficult divorce and fighting for custody of my son; here, I was in my element mingling with performers and artists. I had one day off and my mum and dad brought my son to see me and I remember heading off to the castle with him on my shoulders carrying a sword filled with Smarties, battling our way through the crowds and street performers.

We got some great reviews and everything was looking good for *Sam and Cy* at that point. But even though our show had done well we still came out in debt and were unable to pay our agent. This led to disillusionment with the whole comedy industry – and the pressure of performing, working and family life meant that we just ran out of steam and, although Uncle Dan kindly paid off our debt, we were unable to build on our success by returning the following year.

—— *Leslie* ——

There are sports that require fit and agile minds. I found one to exercise my youthful intellect, but gave it up in favour of the skill of transferring voice to paper.

Chess was my teenage mind sport. It's a predictive game, where the players calculate long chains of moves, often at great speed, and it helps with planning, memory and Einstein-like *imaginary experiments*. It also has its own aesthetic logic, relying on accuracy and small advantages built up through flawless play, but touched with fire. For me, it was a dramatic art. I wanted to create unusual positions on the board, placing pieces where they *shouldn't go* and executing beautifully memorable moves that contradicted all expectations. So part of me was playing against the limits of the game, searching for surprising combinations – and the act of seeing ahead to create these climatic moments was a kind of magic.

There was another part of me that wanted to win. Chess is full of pressure, and very personal. I'd learned that from remarks by Bobby Fischer about *weakies*, and the story of Aron Nimzowitsch leaping onto a table and shouting, "Why must I lose to this idiot?" What I didn't appreciate, as I searched for my brilliancy, was the importance of screening out mistakes – because one blunder can be fatal. So blocking and anticipation is often more important than conjuring up a surprise attack.

But avoidance play wasn't for me. I wasn't going to outlast my opponent, partly because my stamina wasn't good. To sit in silence with a tight chest and both legs shaking felt like going to the dentist. It hurt; it went on for hours; there were no excuses.

So why did I study chess, often for hours a day?

Firstly, it allowed me to adopt the mantle of expert. Chess was a specialist subject, a rarefied thought bubble so private and arcane that it made me unchallengeable. Secondly, I could dream of playing the world's top grandmasters and defeating them. Thirdly, and most importantly, it acted as a compensation for my lack of worldly nous. So in a group of boys I was last to catch on to double entendres, in class I'd miss the point or answer the wrong question, and on the playing field my moves were random panicky air-swipes leading to ridicule and falls.

Chess, for me, was the beautiful game. Certain positions were symmetrical, others were open, there were patterns with balance and directional feel; it was a fine art with its own established conventions and visual effects. But what continued to fascinate me – to the detriment of my over-the-board play – were the counter-intuitive moves that sidestep convention taking the game to unexpected places. So my interest was in gambits, crazy positions and new discoveries – any line, in fact, that was showy and took the game *outside the book*.

It's the game in the head that interests me now. Once you go beyond the basic rules, chess takes on a teasing, cat and mouse quality. So chess problems are a psychological contest where the solutions are whodunit-like, and the least likely move is the answer. The key move is far fetched, unorthodox and anti-positional. Sometimes it's a self-block or a waiting move. At other times the problem has an apparently *winning* try that will fail, or an *obvious* mating pattern that doesn't work. Sometimes it's mazy, with different answers to each defence, and in some problems it's a retreat, or a complete switch of tactics. So the problem tests out the limits of conventional play, reading people's minds to find their blind spots and shake up routine thinking.

Over the board, play is less cut and dried. There are traps and swindles and time scrambles where it's staying calm that counts. Even when defeat seems certain, the trick is not to give anything away. In other games, the aim is to stir up complications and blitz through, choosing moves that keep the other side guessing. Anything goes, whether it's playing for territory, making use of unusual openings, or grinding out a win by following a well known analysis. But whatever the method, it's a dance where every move counts, and where there are no second chances.

In the end I stopped playing chess. I was more interested in personal relationships than abstract brain teasers. It wasn't enough. People were more subtle and varied, friendships were more important, and writing was the mind sport I wanted to practise.

Sue

Ways to make a story ~

In the garden, with a costume, a wigwam, invisible ink or a tree. And a brother.

Write it with a sparkler through the dark.

Dance it till it feels real.

With something small but beautiful, like a petal or a stone that comes from another world or time.

Give it to the waves as a secret when it's too cold to swim.

Fly with the birds.

Imagine you're someone brand new, and find a way to be a hero.

Be a mummy and tell it until baby sleeps.

Take a sword to scare a baddie away.

Move cardboard people across a cardboard stage (and sing the *Thunderbirds* theme before each scene) and give them all different voices.

In episodes, starring Twinkle Troll or Josephine.

With a cake and a party for a doll's birthday.

Use bricks for a house and make a surprise happen in it.

Turn the stairs into a bus and drive to exciting stops.

Capture it on paper with drawings.

Ways to make a story funny ~
Make Daddy a policeman on a bridge saying STOP and just keep running past until he chases you and you have to hide or be turned upside down.
Let your brother tell it.

——— *Cy* ———

Leslie: I know Uncle Dan was an important figure in your life. Can you tell us about him, please?
Cy: Uncle Dan, aka The Soup-maker, was a huge inspiration to me. He had his own art studio and had given up working as an engineer at Ford's to become an artist.
He was a true bohemian, extremely eccentric and full of wild energy. On a night shortly after my son was born we went on a Nekyia or *Night Sea Voyage* from the town into the countryside, crossing  the river of fire that was the motorway and stopping to talk with the Houyhnhnms in the moonlight; we faced our demons in the woods where he struck a skull-faced tree and we chanted and danced and howled into the night sky in an ancient, magical ceremony of our own to welcome and protect the new child who had entered the world. Dan always encouraged and supported my work as a visual artist, poet, writer and performer. I think he's come along to see me perform more than anyone else and I painted a large portrait of him over a period of six months when I had become homeless and he took me in.

He suffered with his mental health throughout his life and the portrait was a collaboration between us, with him telling me how he felt and me weaving his nausea and fear into the painting. He had some of my artwork framed and put on his wall, and he spent time reading and discussing my creative writing, usually over gin and tonic. He died recently and I miss him more than I can say. It was a discussion with him and my son when we went on a camping trip to Norfolk that led me to write the short *Sam and Cy* film *Tillington Hills*. Apparently it's a type of cider – but my son thought it sounded like the name of a Victorian explorer and the three of us went off on a journey imagining his adventures. The notes from that conversation were the bones of my eventual screenplay.

I remember walking into the kitchen one morning to find him cooking one of his many fry-ups and him turning to me with a look of almost blissful serenity and saying, "There's something strangely relaxing about cooking sausages" – a line I immediately scribbled down in my notepad. Dan was always a goldmine for such phrases in my character comedy.

I once went over with my son, Dylan, to Auntie Sarah's bright yellow custard house for a *Carpet Picnic* with her and Uncle Dan. We discovered he'd cooked the biggest pile of sausages imaginable. He'd obviously been feeling stressed. As a five-year old boy, my son was of course delighted, and he and Dan snaffled them down. Afterwards the two of them decided on a trampoline session on the bed, at which point Uncle Dan threw up, much to my son's fascination. He'd never seen an adult unapologetically break the rules with so much abandon.

Dan loved cooking for others – looking after people. But sometimes an artistic fever would grip him and scupper the dinner plans. I recall going round for a roast dinner and Sarah explaining that Dan had kidnapped the chicken and retired to his studio and wasn't to be disturbed. Hours later he emerged excitedly and turned the chicken upside down on the kitchen counter. When a Perspex ball fell out of its arse he grinned. "Right! Let's cook this thing!" He'd been taking photographs of the inside of the chicken, fascinated by the shapes the veins and blood vessels made.

One Christmas day as I arrived home after visiting my son I discovered him like some crazed anti-Santa butchering a roadkill deer in my back garden. We ate it together for Christmas dinner, but realising we had no gravy Dan produced Frank Zappa's album *Lumpy Gravy* from the back of his Land Rover to accompany it. I left Dan with the remains of the roadkill whilst I visited Yorkshire and when we returned my mum knocked at the front door. Shortly afterwards a naked Dan answered, covered from head to toe in blood and clutching his hunting knife.

Mum didn't bat an eyelid.

"Hello Dan!"

"Hello Eve!" Big friendly smile. "I'm just skinning my deer in the bath ... hmmm ..." He looked disappointed. "I was hoping to make a jacket but it's gone a bit wrong and I think I've only got enough to make a small hat."

Dan enjoyed being silly and childish. He loved Monty Python and the film *Team America* and when he first discovered it he watched it over and over crying with laughter, particularly at the vomiting scene. A good dose of Dan went into a lot of my comedy scripts. His favourite sketch involved Sam and me leaping around pretending to be apes in dress suits. Dan would howl with laughter remembering the stunned expressions of the audience. I think it was the juxtaposition of the *civilised outfit* with the bow ties and the sight of us grooming each other for tics and grunting. Dan was our official photographer for many years. As you can imagine, photo shoots with Dan were often unorthodox and at times dangerous. On one such shoot he insisted Sam and I strip half naked and crawl backwards into a rusty old furnace beneath a huge brick chimney on the grounds of a psychiatric hospital. In one of the photos as the skin is scraped off Sam's back you can see him looking at Dan thinking "Are you insane?!" The picture was great though and we used it on our posters and it was published in the paper to advertise our show *Sam and Cy – Unhinged* and that went on to be the name of our Edinburgh show.

—— Leslie ——

My grandmother used to say, "It's a performance." By that she meant a task that was difficult and complicated and needed a real effort. *A performance* was fiddly, something you had to work at, and didn't make much sense until you'd got the hang of it. It took practice and persistence and often happened when you were least expecting it.

She *performed* for guests, placing them at the table and serving tea with fancy cakes, then insisting loudly that they must clear their plates. Afterwards, she needed to sit down for a minute to catch her breath. "Eh, what a performance," she said, shaking.

The phrase wasn't hers. It belonged to anyone who'd *not had it easy* and needed to say so, loudly, for the benefit of an imaginary audience.

For me as a child my grandmother's words had a number of hidden meanings:

a. Behind her bravado she was out of her depth, struggling and up against it, at an unfair disadvantage. Her words were an appeal.
b. Said with vehemence, the phrase was a protest against clever-clever people like teachers and officials who did things the hard way.

c. Used by my dad, "It's such a performance," was depressively angry.
d. Later, I linked the phrase with others like, *It's such a carry on* and *A right palaver*. They were all short-fuse statements ready to explode.
e. Still later I discovered *a performance* could mean making a fuss.

My grandparents on the other side led a choir. My grandfather, a romantic Gigli-type tenor, sang and conducted while my granny accompanied on piano and organ. Whatever they performed, it had to be near-perfect. Their repertoire ranged from Gilbert and Sullivan and Geordie songs to operatic arias and *The Messiah*. They worked for months, drilling the choir on diction, counting bars and breathing. Thanks to them each performance was a show, a dressed-up spectacle with grandpa conducting and granny at his side, harmonising. For them, it was all about timing, discipline and following the score.

As a child who loved being photographed, I enjoyed performing to camera. In any family group I'd be at the front smiling as if it was my birthday. Being caught on camera was my chance to take centre stage. It gave me a puckish feel as if I was perfect. Here I was with a starring role; a shy only child who enjoyed being seen. It made up for school where I ducked out of sight, giving way in queues and standing at the back for class photos. On the games field I was the substitute no one wanted. And in the classroom I sat in a corner with my eyes down saying nothing.

But was I really performing? Yes and no. Being *me* certainly felt like a calculated act. I played the boy who pushed himself forward to hog the camera and the schoolboy blanking his expression to dodge the gang. I was both and neither, actor and audience, show-off and victim, imitating myself in an attempt to fit in.

But on my own, when I became the secret girlie *me*, the real self in hiding wasn't giving a performance. That was a state of mind.

Sue

Once there was a girl who was scared of her face in the water. She blew so it wobbled away but then it came back again. "That's not me," she said, and went to climb a tree. But the tree was magic and its leaves were made of gold so she saw her face shining in them. She rattled the branches till the face broke. Then she jumped down and went to see her friend Emerald the horse but when she fed him she saw her face in his eyes.

She let go of the reins and ran to hide in a cave. She sat and cried in the dark. Then she heard a soft snuffling sound and the swish of a tail. Emerald nuzzled her and she knew he loved her. She climbed on his warm, velvet back and trotted out into the sunshine. Away she rode, over the hills and across the river and she didn't look down. But when night came she looked at the stars and she smiled. "That's me," she said.

Cy

Leslie: So what happened after the Edinburgh Festival?
Cy: I was lucky enough to be spotted at a gig in London by a film producer who gave me my first role in a feature. It

was definitely the biggest budget film I've ever been in, and of course, because my life always seems to take on a surreal slant, I played a manic game show host in little more than a codpiece in a film about a giant boxing shrimp. I had a driver who picked me up and took me to the studio each day, where I was spray-tanned and put in gold lamé hot pants, a conch codpiece, gold cowboy boots and a laurel wreath. I then stood onstage in a huge purpose-built arena before an audience of extras who were paid to laugh and applaud my every word as I introduced a Giant Animatronic Shrimp. That one experience did teach me about continuity and the importance of keeping your performance consistent in each shot. The first time I stepped in front of the camera I gave it my all, waving manically and striding about. Then I heard, "Cut." Then, "Go again." Then, "No, no stop! In the last take you went over there and waved your left arm, then your right and ..." I soon realised that less is more in terms of gesture and that you had to remember your mark and keep to it. I also realised that film acting was a completely different process from being on the stage and that you have to do the same thing, in pretty much exactly the same way, over and over again. It was a steep but quick learning curve and a great experience.

—— *Leslie* ——

We filmed *Heaven's Rage* – based on my book of the same title – in a sunny wood on the outskirts of Watford. We'd taken a winding, potholed road to get there, passing through stretches of fenced-off wasteland and scrubby undergrowth, then a concrete tunnel beneath a motorway, to arrive at cottages surrounded by sunspots and greenery. The drive was short but varied, changing from town to country, from noise and action to enclosed space, from dusty main roads to a shaded country lane. It was as if we'd taken a back route to a forgotten childhood territory where anything might happen.

There were five of us: Mark Crane, the director; James Melrose on camera; Daniel Dunn child-actor; Daniel's mother, Amanda; and me. Arriving in three cars, we parked by a fence just beyond a boarded-up cottage and James unloaded his equipment. With the help of Mark he carried a lens bag, a ladder-like tripod, two large stands and a heavy black camera to a place opposite the cottage. Setting up the equipment took several minutes; when fully assembled it looked like an imaginary AI machine.

We'd filmed one scene the night before. Using blackout curtains to seal off Mark's living room, we'd created a dream-world with James in one half, taking pictures of me behind a table, wearing a white shirt and black suit and tie. Mark's wife, Sheelagh, was there, watching from the side, while Mark himself was teasing out wire wool from a package, coiling the black, fibrous material into a wine glass. His thin, agile hands moved quickly, shaping it to fit.

"A trick I learned in special effects," he said.

Mark struck a match.

"Let's see how it burns," he said.

When the flame touched the wool, the red glow spread in patches, reaching the ends and curling like singed hair.

"Oh, I love that, it's so magical," said Sheelagh.

Reflected in glass, the wool looked like a red-hot mineral.

The drink scene took the rest of the evening. Mark directed, offering verbal prompts, checking his storyboard and rustling up props. His role, as répétiteur, was to tweak everything. Sheelagh had taken charge of the metal wool, which she tugged and smoothed into layers. James, carrying the camera in a fireman's lift, was adjusting focus and calling "Action."

The action of the drink scene involved me striking bunches of matches and raising them to my face. The air felt charged, as if I was holding a blowtorch. With the glass burning by my elbow, I was inside a restricted territory, a kind of lit-up frame in space. It was odd and slightly disturbing – dangerous even – because viewed back on camera, the fire seemed to be eating my skin. I was in another world, a chthonic figure absorbed by his own obsession.

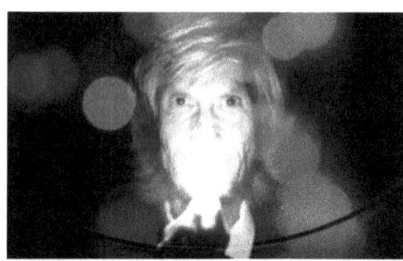

Filming in the woods next morning was a different story. Watching the process, I saw myself through another person's eyes. Mark directed as Daniel pushed along an overgrown path to stand in front of the boarded-up cottage, waving. Wearing my tie and jacket, he looked like a fresh-faced version of my former self, or the child I might have been if I'd grown up in 2017 instead of the 1950s.

At thirteen, Daniel was an experienced actor whose curly-haired innocence was matched by his adult understanding. He was camp, affectionate and worldly-wise. Physically, he was fluid in an intermediate way, so his body was boyish but rounded while his face had both charm and a male directness – he was straight and attentive and gently playful. Several times during the shoot I thought, "If only I'd been like that!"

In the course of a day's filming we were scratched by brambles and stung by nettles as we carried our props – including a bed frame, mattress and sheets – over ditches and dead branches into quiet forest clearings. The sets we created were carefully put together; they had clarity and edge plus a deliberate wildness – matching the film's clean surfaces and surprising juxtapositions. At the centre of each, posed and positioned by Mark, was Daniel playing me: a boy-girl waking in bed in a forest fantasy, or tied by bullies to a tree wearing a red dress, as in my short story *A Dream*.

We broke for lunch at 2.30 p.m. By then I'd been crouched on a log too hungry to do anything, until Mark noticed and sent me to his car with the keys.

"There's some fruit in the boot," he'd called. "Please help yourself."

At the car, after stuffing down a banana and three apples, I chatted to Amanda, who'd volunteered to guard the unused equipment. She told me about Daniel: the roles he'd played, his gay self-acceptance, his close friendships and support at school. As we talked, the sun shone in pools and streaks across the forest floor. When our conversation stopped, birdsong took over. The air was warm and still, and the light was high. It was quiet, we were there waiting in the woods and the film was progressing ...

—— *Cy* ——

Leslie: Am I right in thinking that your role as a game show host led on to parts in horror films?

Cy: Yes. Soon afterwards I began my long collaboration with independent horror writer and director Pat Higgins. I'd appeared a few times at Pat's comedy club in Southend, so when he was shooting his first feature *Trashhouse* and needed a last minute stand-in for the mysterious *Agent Allen* a friend suggested me, and Pat, remembering my performance, took me on. I had to learn my lines in an evening and be on set the next day. I loved it. The difference with low-budget and independent film making is that everyone has to pitch in, and Pat Higgins creates a friendly family-type environment on shoots with people painting scenery and mixing up fake blood while others pop out to get snacks and pick up last-minute props. He's an incredibly nice chap and that really helps. Over the years I have been in six of Pat's features and one short. Weirdly the film *KillerKiller* was actually shot in the psychiatric institution where I had had my first job. The old redbrick Victorian asylum was now deserted and builders were beginning to gut its interior to make luxury flats, but some wards were still intact. It was strange being back there and walking down the echoing corridors. It certainly made a great location though, and Director of Photography, Al Ronald, made the most of it. It was there we met, sharing an off-set cigarette break and our love of crazy comedy ... and so my second double act was born. Shortly afterwards we recorded our first series of podcasts.

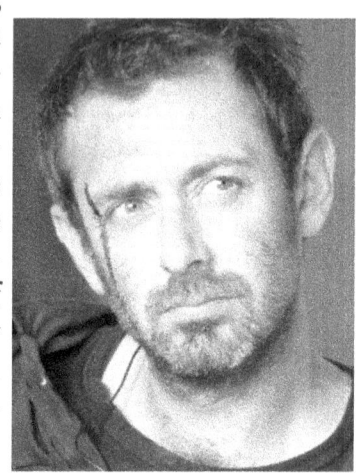

—— *Leslie* ——

On set with Mark and James over that weekend, I experienced the full, behind-the-scenes impact of film-making. It resembled trekking, weighed down by kit, on a winding path where each stretch could take anything from a few minutes to several hours. The kit involved costumes, props, stands, lights, batteries, lenses, laptops and numerous other bits and pieces including food, drink, gaffer tape and call sheets. It was easy to leave something behind, drop it, or get lost – the latter involving cars separated, chasing each other or long waits while Mark went scouting. The locations took hours to fix or disguise or set up outdoors, with problems over lighting and composition; while the actions involved repeated takes of the same short scene. Coupled with the demanding schedule, exacting photography and so few helpers, it could only lead to long waits, sudden switches and lots of confusion ... Indie filming, I learned, was a life on the brink, ever-shifting, lived out of bags, and chaotic.

But the dream kept us going. So the mud-mound where we filmed in the local park doubled as a dry stream bed, and the woods we used – a strip on the edge of a busy motorway – became part of untouched, rural England. Even indoors, we dressed the set with fake floorboards, unreal lighting and full-length mirrors. Anything was possible, and each scene was a try-on and a lucky-dip experiment – though it was also an escape to a different mind-set. Because our film was about vision and deep psychology. It was a hall of mirrors where we continually cheated reality, framing the shots to trick our audience and set up their dream.

In fact, there were two films. There was the non-linear adaptation of my memoir *Heaven's Rage*, and another, more domestic story, involving my day-to-day relationship. This second story was about love and long-term commitment and the gap between feelings and life, because to be on the shoot I'd had to leave Sue, my wife, recovering from day surgery with pre-prepared food and a couple of scheduled visits. It seemed typically male and disloyal but she insisted I went, telling me she'd manage. So I left her, although I knew she feared being alone, and during the filming I received more than one text telling me how ill she was.

So the two films ran on, side by side, as if they were the same story being shown in different languages or different chapters taken from the same book. In my Sue-film the location was the bedroom, the shots were of hands on pills and spills on trays, while the dialogue was fitful. There were moments where I sat on the bed and we chatted about news and friendships and Sue's latest symptoms, and other times when we talked, between long pauses, about how to manage pain. To an outsider it might have seemed quite couply, with me playing nurse and Sue eating or resting, but the hidden doubts were there, running around our heads.

Firstly, there was the issue of earning a *pass out*, a practice I'd been used to as a parent but involving a lot of extra work, some of it for show. Secondly, and more importantly, I was struggling with a fatiguing condition that the doctors couldn't diagnose. Thirdly there was Sue's fear of abandonment, that illness made her unattractive and would drive me away. Fourthly we were in love and unprepared for what felt like separation. Fifthly, and crucially, Sue was ill.

So the slow-paced Sue-film was a documentary, leaving the audience to guess at the actors' moods. It was a series of stills, a quiet, nagging companion piece to *Heaven's Rage*, running on regardless with its own private fears and internal imaginings that threatened to undermine everything.

— *Sue* —

The girl watched the darkness around her. Now that she had her own bedroom, being alone felt strange, as if she was Gerda separated from Kay and that made the world a different kind of story. The silence was fuller and blacker, and hid things. She reminded herself of the shapes with their ordinary names: the sloping wardrobe in the eaves, her door onto the landing, bookshelves Daddy had made for her along the wall, the cupboard that was a Sindy house on two floors. Not that she played with dolls now – but she could, if she chose and didn't tell, and there were never any ghouls or witches in those games, only weddings and meals and Patch getting up to mischief that made the others laugh.

Somewhere on her desk, Sparkle the lion troll sat with his round eyes on her, but the dark had taken their shine. She missed the bedtime magic now that he was no longer a prince, just a toy Mummy dusted. Tonight whenever she closed her eyes, the Ogre was there, the one she'd seen on Nana and Pop's television that Christmas when she was little. Its mouth swallowed its cruel face and out of it roared a laugh with evil filling it. Somehow it had got inside her and it might be there for ever, because how could she forget? So much scarier than a lion could ever be, it was nearly human but not, and that was the worst kind of being. Was that how people could be, even if they wore shirts with ties, and suits and polished shoes? Was that why some grownups believed in the Devil, even though Mummy and Daddy said it was make-believe, like Father Christmas?

Daddy thought the world was too evil for her to know. That was why he wouldn't let her look at the paper he read on the train home. Last time she'd found it and quietly tried to see why, he'd caught her and said softly, "No, darling. Please." He wasn't cross but sad, as if the news made him unhappy. But other people watched it at teatime on their televisions. Was it because he cared more about things that happened in America and Africa and Russia than the other parents, or really, really loved her – even more than they loved their children? It was a bit like keeping something precious – a petal or jewel or shell – safe in a matchbox with tissue.

She told herself the only living thing upstairs with her was her brother, dreaming – of cricket or chocolates, or being an astronaut maybe. The Ogre was hers because it had swallowed her too when its great mouth gaped open like a cave that was darker than this, darker than space. Its laugh shook everything inside her chest where her heart was.

If she used her torch and read under the blankets, she could block it out for now, with Malcolm Saville or Jennings, or girls riding horses and saving some kind of day. Not *A Little Princess* because it was her favourite, but she cried too much for night-time when Sara's daddy didn't come – and when he did. Mummy said she shouldn't but she found the switch on the torch from her last Christmas stocking and lit the spines on the shelf enough to recognise the titles. But it was so hard to choose and she'd finished three library books this week.

She must go back after school tomorrow and find some more. And maybe she should write one, about a girl who had nightmares but something wonderful happened to make them go away …

—— *Leslie* ——

Shooting *Heaven's Rage* took longer than expected. The overrun was needed to work on Mark's sketches and shape them into finished cinema. It was a fiddly, trial-and-error job, shifting and changing everything before running and re-running the camera through several takes, all of them requiring further changes before moving on to the next.

"I won't shoot shit," James declared, as he waved me back and forth until I was standing just where he wanted, head-on to the camera.

"Step back a bit," he said quietly, gazing down the viewfinder.

"Forward again," he called.

"Hold it there," he added, gently, "still as you can."

By the time we'd filmed it, a few seconds of footage had taken nearly an hour to shoot.

It took six days, working twelve hours a day, to film *Heaven's Rage*. There were stops and starts and occasional disagreements with James as *down-to-earth craftsman*, challenging Mark as *arthouse dreamer* to explain the aim of each shot. In this debate, while James stood for realism, Mark wanted poetry and surprise. The result was an argument, gentle at first but escalating later, in which I played peacemaker, asking about the industry and their stories of joshing and abuse. In fact I didn't need to. As friends and co-creatives, Mark and James were quite unlike the film-set bullies they talked about, and the tensions that surfaced were the result of tiredness and lack of a crew.

But watching back the footage was a lift. It was as if we were on location in the mind of the reader, seeing for real the characters in my book.

By the last full day of filming we were quicker: debating less, doing more. We felt freer and less pressured because the difficult scenes were over and what remained seemed doable. So we put on a spurt, James called, "Action," and suddenly, before we knew it, the end was in sight. We shot the final scene by a street lamp, surrounded by hedges on a warm night with moths in the air.

It was there, at the centre of a softly-lit circle where four paths met, that we worked on the *reveal*. It came in one take. As my head went back, I reached up, and the camera closed on my outline in a dress. Inside the child and the suited man were burning up; outside was me: the cross-dressed author. And behind that was Sue, walking with me into sunlight, speaking of love and calling me her beautiful boy ...

—— *Sue* ——

The grinding noise was over now but the garden still smelt of wood. There was a fine dusting around the sliced stump where the tree used to make shade. The girl thought of a painting she'd seen in The Tate Gallery, of the boy Jesus in the carpenter's workshop. Daddy would be proud that she remembered the artist's name too: Sir John Everett Millais. But she wouldn't mention it. She wouldn't say anything in case the words were wrong. She just stood on the step down from the living room and watched.

Daddy wasn't browning in the deck chair, or mowing the lawn, or looking at the red geraniums gathering in a crowd alongside her. "What a colour!" he'd said last year. "Scarlet, carmine or vermillion?" "Scarlet," she'd decided. That would have been a more beautiful name than Susan, and fitted a heroine better.

Now he sat on the grass, with splinters around him, and his knees up in front of his chest. His arms hugged his legs and his head was down, but not for long because a moment later he gazed up at the space the tree had filled, as if it was a scar that hurt. The girl knew he was crying even before a sound broke out. It wasn't loud but deep and shaky. His body rattled softly, like the branches of the tree used to do when it was windy. Inside the girl the stiffness started, filling her. It was what happened to her breathing when it made no difference how much she loved him.

Mummy was behind her now. She laid a hand on her shoulder and whispered, "Daddy's heartbroken, darling. He blames himself. But we had no choice."

The girl knew about the roots that had grown in secret, and webbed out towards the foundations. Daddy had drawn the house on his board at the office so he called it a mistake building too close to the tree. But no one could have dreamed that it was creeping secretly towards them, day by day, week by week, while they ate and played and slept. She imagined the roots like arms with muscles and fists – breaking through the earth and shattering the concrete to lift up the house and tilt it like a ship on a wave. It wasn't really frightening, because it was harder to believe in than the Ogre who used to give her bad dreams when she was small.

She was too grown-up for a swing now anyway.

Mummy went slowly out across the grass and sat down beside Daddy. He turned towards her and his face was wet, and creased out of shape. Mummy reached her arm across his back and he leaned towards her. The girl couldn't hear what she said to him but he kept on crying.

She wished he'd stop now. He preferred the garden to other people. It was his place to breathe after London and the train. It was his painting. But his heart had more cracks than it should and that scared her more than roots could ever do. Why couldn't he forgive himself? The sun was bright and the geraniums didn't care.

It was just a tree.

—— *Cy* ——

Leslie: Tell us about your podcasts with Al Ronald and what followed.

Cy: Al and I put together a series of podcasts, working all night in a small sound-proofed shed at the bottom of a friend's garden. From that we went live, picking out the best sketches to perform at the Camden Fringe Festival.

The festival stage was a tiny space and we had a plethora of different characters and crazy props, including a hippo-head mask that I'd made out of mudrock. Unfortunately, although the mask captured the hippo's sad expression, it weighed a ton and had no eyeholes to speak of. We had to quick-change behind a curtain strung up in the corner of the room, leading to a lot of frantic scrabbling about. To be honest, I think this really added to the manic energy of the show.

We moved from there to filming our first pilot, *Wrong Way Round,* a spoof of a popular reality TV series, and *The Cracks are Showing*, made with the help of *Mighty Boosh* producer Ali Macphail. We were pretty excited at this point but unfortunately got knocked back by another producer. *The Cracks* involved Al Ronald and me locked up in my house, taking turns to film each other as I played his nemesis. At times we both thought we were going insane! The work is very autobiographical, with Al's character embodying our experience as struggling artists in the modern world. During *The Cracks are Showing* Al, under my direction, had to bury himself naked in the snow and climb a mountain with a ten-foot aerial on his head. In our next film together, *Chinese Burns*, he set out to get his revenge. I remember a freezing October night shoot in a car park where, wearing only a shirt, I had to be repeatedly hit over the head with a tennis ball in a sock, dragged around unconscious and then handcuffed. On the same shoot my ex-wife also had the pleasure of smashing a number of sugar-glass vases over my head! My favourite Al Ronald film was *Harriet's War* in which I played PC Jones, a lovely, likeable, innocent character. My dad had been a village policeman so it was weird

looking at myself in the mirror with an imperial moustache and police uniform. Al insisted, in case of retakes, that I keep the moustache I'd grown for a month after the shoot, which raised some eyebrows picking my son up from school and doing the weekly shop.
Leslie: And I believe you've turned your hand to film illustration as well?
Cy: Over the years I've provided artwork for Pat Higgins' films – my favourite being the opening sequence to *Hellbride* in which I actually got to voiceover my own drawings. I also painted a Hieronymus Bosch-style picture for *The Devil's Music* and drew some pictures for a new sequence in Al Ronald's *Jesus vs The Messiah*.

—— *Leslie* ——

I'm lying on my side in a darkened studio with lights and a camera pointed at my bare back. Christoffer is taking the pictures, directed by Andreas and Dagmara. The studio is in Aarhus, Denmark, I'm naked, and the film, called *Landscapes*, puts together close-up images of seven LGBTQ people over 60.

It's a four-hour shoot, first across my back then tight on my chest, moving to my hand and finally to my upper body and face. While the camera pans through smoke effects and I'm in the picture, the film crew are exclaiming how beautiful it looks. Dagmara calls the session "funky". It's as if they're sightseers in a gallery being constantly surprised and astonished by the artwork they see there.

As I stretch out, the words *truth to material* pass through my head. I think of Jean Arp's mixed organic/inorganic forms and picture myself *inside* my body image. I feel as if I'm a figure in *The Garden of Earthly Delights*.

So why are we doing this? Possibly because it's funded and will be shown at a gender festival, maybe as the beginning of a cultural change, or perhaps just because we can …

—— *Cy* ——

Leslie: Would you like to bring us up to date on your current work?
Cy: *The Electric Head* recorded a series of live radio shows at Watford Museum and on stages in the town centre for Watford Live! I've also voiced Molly Brown's comic animations, and was lucky enough to have her animate one of my monologues, *Lenny the Lobster* and a comic poem I wrote called *The Furniture of Pain* which I performed trying to channel my childhood hero Christopher Lee. I really enjoy working with Molly and have recently voiced her latest animation, a spoof of *This Morning* set in the afterlife which involved a manic performance as the host Philip Schofield! Her short, in which I performed *My Crazy Hand*, won the 2018 Golden Trellick Award for Best Comedy at the Portabello Film Festival. I think we share a surreal and at times macabre sense of humour. In the last few years I've returned to the stage, playing two characters in *Shadow Town* by Mark Crane and a psychopathic serial killer in his *Tick-Tock*. Mark is a great director and a real perfectionist, who always gets a good performance out of his actors. I've also been lucky enough to work with

The Art of Disappearing, an immersive theatre company, on their wonderful piece *The Lost Room*. I got to play an eccentric professor for an entire week at the Bethnal Green Museum of Childhood, welcoming 'adventurers' into a magical world.

—— *Leslie* ——

I'm on my way to shoot *Landscapes*, boarding a plane at Stanstead Airport. To reach my flight I walk down a winding concourse between open shop fronts selling luxury perfumes, make-up and jewellery. Everything appears to be rah-rah-rah. It seems we're living in a land of milk and honey; either that or it's Christmas all the time. There are young, glamorous assistants on both sides holding out cards and free give-aways. I've a feeling, because I'm wearing women's clothes, they think I'm going to sample something. In fact, I'm seeing the shopping mall through the eyes of displaced people and other have-nots. It's a fake fairy tale, a pretence that everything's hunky-dory. And while I can see that the women are all beautiful, I know they're under heavy manners. They *are* their tight clothes and eye shadow and tinted mascara, because they're off-the-peg examples of what they're selling. And behind their dolled-up appearance they're overdressed, and their wares are placebos.

After boarding and take-off, our plane climbs over houses and fields, through cloud and out into sun. It's a cheap flight, the cabin is crowded and there isn't much legroom. I'm sitting in the middle of a row, wondering whether to ask the man on my right to let me out to the toilet. The man is 35-ish, wearing denim, and plugged into what I imagine to be music, possibly instrumental. His headphones are like cannula; they make him oblivious and hard to reach.

I ask him, of course, after wondering how to get his attention and measuring his reaction when I do. He doesn't say anything, simply moving out and in, reversing the process when I return. He doesn't appear to notice, but I have to wonder if he's making a point about what I'm wearing. I imagine – absurdly – taking the gangway as my catwalk and displaying my dress. It's blue with tassels and crocheted arms and I wear it with leggings and Mary Jane shoes. It makes me feel comfortable, and though the cabin is crowded, I'm protected in my own quiet space, just as I am.

When the plane descends my ears hurt as if I'm ill.

Before the shoot I chat with Dagmara and Andreas in an Aarhus café. We sit by a large picture window looking out on cyclists, painted buildings and casually-dressed shoppers. It's an urban world, carefully constructed, with everything in place. So this is Denmark, I think: close-knit, urban, trusting – though Dagmara and Andreas warn me about the flipside: the *Folkeparti* with its popularist agenda.

We talk performance. When I ask about *Landscapes*, Dagmara tells a story – how she and Andreas met at art college and put on shows, mainly experimental, continuing since as artists and dancers, organising events and community projects. "It's about working with people," she says, turning to Andreas, "and continually reinventing yourself."

Andreas grins. "You mean like this?" he asks, pointing to his beard.

Dagmara smiles. "Oh yes, *Mr Man*."

I understand the joke but not why he's changed. I'd seen him on the website in ultra-high heels and make-up, covered with blood and flowers and dancing like Salome. I'd assumed that was why they'd invited me. He'd been wildly, defiantly arty and gender-queer. But in the flesh, Andreas is quite different. Short and compact, wearing jeans and a jacket, he looks like an average, dressed-down student; an easy-going guy without too much *femme*.

"I used to be all-girl, everywhere," he says, lengthening his vowels, "but then *this* came over me."

"Anyway," he continues, "it's much easier now on the street."

— Cy —

Leslie: So how would you sum up your experience of being an actor?

Cy: I think I could quite happily live in a world of make-believe, being everything from Robin Hood to super heroes to cowboys with my son in trips to the woods, and improvising and performing with Sam and Al. In my creative writing and visual art I have often explored identity and the boundaries between fiction and reality. In the modern world with the advent of the smartphone and other technologies, and the rise of reality TV, we see that border becoming ever more blurred. As Arthur Cravan said, "Dream your life with great care instead of living it merely as an amusement."

―― *Leslie* ――

Afterwards, on our way to the shoot, I enjoy the sunshine. It's always easier walking outdoors in a dress when you're with others, and Dagmara and Andreas are my guardians and psychopomps.

As we leave the busy shopping streets, I glance up at the sky. It's an untouched canvas. We talk about the filming.

"You know what to expect, yes?" Dagmara asks gently.

I do mainly, I say, but ask about the ending.

Andreas answers. "That's when we go inside. But we don't, of course. We'll close in on your mouth, but only a bit. The camera does the rest."

"Non-invasive, then?"

"It's not an operation. Promise."

"But on screen? What do the audience see?"

"That'll be the beach shots. Taken in North Denmark."

I express my surprise and ask about the beach. They tell me it's a desert: out of this world, and very beautiful. I think of Surrealist pictures and the work of Franz Marc. Above, the sky is a clear bare screen.

We continue walking, chatting about ideas. Dagmara and Andreas guide me past statues and benches, across a planted square and in through a door to enter a shadowy area with a low stage and a darkened auditorium. Christoffer joins us, switching on the spotlights. Their beams spread evenly on an exercise mattress at the front of the auditorium. Behind that the light fades from grey into black. It makes the room seem cave-like and unreal. When the filming begins I visualise the journey I've been through to get here …

—— *Cy* ——

Leslie: Could you add something more about the importance of Arthur Cravan to you, please?

Cy: Arthur Cravan was a poet and Dadaist performer at the beginning of the 20th Century who challenged the audience's preconceptions. His performances included shooting himself and challenging the Heavyweight Champion of the World to a boxing match. I have met a lot of artists over the years who embodied his sense of anarchy and willingness to risk everything for their art: none more so than Russell Brand and Uncle Dan. Those artists have a certain electricity and mania about them – they are both fascinating and at times terrifying. I admire greatly artists who stay true to their vision, and directors Al Ronald and Pat Higgins certainly have a spark of Cravan in them also. Pat's films are intelligent and question the conventions of film, genre and stereotypes, and I know he has fought hard to bring his vision to the screen on what is often a shoestring budget. Al is the same, he has an uncompromising vision in both his film and comedy work.

—— *Leslie* ——

The film in my head begins on the beach. I can feel the wind against my body, tickling my skin. I'm imagining myself in a swimsuit, the sort worn in secret, taken from a drawer. It's tight and wraps my chest in touchy-feely stuff. I'm stretched and alive; in my own element and breathless. It's as if I've been caught on camera like one of those smooth-faced models I keep hidden in my schoolbag. She's in there, smiling. Later on, I'll carry her inside me, doll-like and invisible. And she's still there: the half-and-half child who poses in the mirror and dreams of being loved.

In the frames that follow, my journey becomes an escape or a quest. It's a high-up adventure over sea and land to arrive at a city where I'm met at the station by Dagmara and Andreas who, without saying anything, shift me to their studio. It's an operating theatre and they're my consultants. As the camera moves slowly across my body to my mouth, it's as if they're voices from the past, God-like and ancestral, talking me through. Suddenly I'm in the dark.

When the light returns, the landscape has changed. It's a bare white beach, where heaven and earth come together. It's before dawn, where light meets dark and new shapes arise. As the camera pulls back the film rolls out like a DNA strip. It stretches away to a long curving landscape with an art-space feel. I'm newborn. Making my way into unexplored territory. Without shadow and genderless ...

The film is made.

ADAPTED FROM LIFE

—— *Cy* ——

When I wore a T-shirt at the Edinburgh Festival saying *This is not my true Identity* – a phrase often used by Sam and me on stage – a man came up to me and said, "I like your T-shirt," to which I replied, "It's not mine."
Who I am does seem like a mystery to me sometimes. But I like to maintain a distance from the person others meet. If I knew who I was, I think I might try too hard to be him and become an exaggerated version of him. That strange man I wake up in bed with every morning.
I'm aware that he's imbued with a spirit of theatricality and romanticism and that there's something frustratingly accidental about him, giving him a certain childlike charm and naivety – some might say a degree of foolishness.

—— *Leslie* ——

We all carry scenes in the head that keep coming back. Mine begin on the beach in childhood. The sands in these pictures are impossibly yellow and the people are ghosts. I see them outlined by the sun, wearing check shirts and dresses: twice life-size with an adult-ish look. They could be living statues. I'm aware of family and how we connect: a fierce, rather distant parental interest like chasing a ball, and the grandparents' shouty voices blown by the wind. The beach is a place of light and shade where everything flows, shifts, dissolves and is fleeting. I'm out there in the glare, running.

My next childhood snapshots are domestic. They're set in strangely bare rooms with cloth pelmets and striped wallpapers that my dad struggled to put up. I can still hear his deep, snorting breaths and muffled exclamations. Just being alone in a room with a *man working* was enough to scare me.

The emptiness of these rooms reminds me of waiting in the clinic for injections. Measuring the distance to doors and windows I'd plot my escape. Perhaps if I could crouch down and change colour to blend in with the furniture? Or develop suckers to climb the walls and wriggle through the ceiling cracks? At other times I'd imagine myself in bed, bound and gagged. I was Houdini at the ready.

Sometimes the house was a ship in the dark. My bedroom was a cabin where I served my time as The Stowaway, listening to the deep ocean sounds piped up from below. There were ghosts moving stealthily, ascending from the dark and sliding at will beneath my bedroom door. I went in fear of angry spirits and chained up mutants in the loft. What would happen if they broke out? And what about the one-eyed giant who'd take off the roof, peer in … and then what might happen?

I built my defences on staying alert. Behind my everyday mask I watched and waited. If I could catch my adversaries I'd squash them like flies. I was the tracker-boy who tapped out coded messages on the walls, in search of allies. Over time, when I'd gathered my forces, I'd make my plans and launch my offensive.

Sometimes, when my bedroom-cell was searched, I lay so flat in bed that my body didn't show. If that didn't work, I'd a disappearing switch inside my brain. I kept it out of view but in one or two pictures there was a tell-tale gap where I'd been standing.

Later, pictured outdoors, I put on my best face. Behind the smile, I was following a story: a back garden battle where snails and spiders fought their corners. When I studied the path, there were bird-snakes and harpies hiding in the cracks. On the lawn, there were dancing wasps and earthworms cut in half. When my mother hung out the clothes, I saw them as winding sheets.

My life in pictures is a waking dream. I'm caught in front of camera, telling my stories to ward off the ghosts. Their bird-shaped shadows are all around. I'm running on the beach with the wind in my face and the sun in my eyes. While I'm running I look straight ahead. The more I do it the less I'm afraid.

—— *Sue* ——

Frinton was cold and the wind blew hard but Pop was there to make it fun. The little girl loved the row of beach huts, painted bright like a Toy Town. Nana and Pop's was clean as a new pin. Its steps up made it like a tree house and there were always biscuits. Because there was a changing space at the back, she didn't have to undress on the sand behind a towel that flapped.

Today Pop had driven them down in the Rover, which was exciting except that she felt sick as usual. "Four wheels don't suit you, Susie," said Pop, "but you're a whizz on two." She wished she was.

Nana had brought cake tins and Tupperware tubs full of food.

"There's nothing left in the larder!" Pop joked. "We're here for the day, not a month."

Nana said it was time for a nice cup of tea from the flask. The girl didn't really like tea but it was too cold for squash. She wished the sea didn't look so grey. It crashed and foamed onto the beach and sometimes the spray seemed to throw salt their way.

"I like the sea fierce!" said Mummy, smiling at it.

So did her brother. In fact, he was peeling off his clothes because his trunks were underneath. He was skinny and springy. He was grinning and didn't shiver. The girl was glad of her anorak even though she hated the shape it gave her.

"It'll be freezing!"

But her brother started down the wooden steps, laughing. Pop just lit his pipe and told him to report back. He used to be a footballer but he was old now.

"Hold on!" cried Daddy, pulling off his shirt. Soon they were running on the sand together. The girl was too slow to catch them so she didn't try. Mummy had brought paper in case she wanted to write or draw, so she sat inside the hut and watched the squealing and shouting as they ran away from the waves. They hopped and gasped. But then her brother waded in up to his waist, and she heard Daddy cry, "Slow down! Where's the fire?"

"Shall we join them?" Mummy asked.

The girl didn't answer because she didn't know. Nana never swam. She always dressed as if she was going for tea at Buckingham Palace so the girl had never seen her skin but it must be wrinkly. Mummy didn't have smart clothes because she didn't care. Her pearls were pretend and popped together.

"I don't want you to miss out and wish you'd given it a try."

"It'll be freezing."

"Yes, but we can thrash about and get warm."

The girl didn't really thrash. She preferred breaststroke with her head up and her mouth closed but water always sloshed in somehow. But she wanted to be with Daddy.

Nana thought it would be sensible to stay in the warm. "I told Pop it wasn't a day for the seaside but he wouldn't listen."

"Oh, the sun will come out and we'll roast later," said Pop.

Mummy said, "Of course it will," and helped the girl get changed into the spotty costume she would like if she had a flatter tummy.

Then she took her hand and they hurried over the sand. The beach was noisier up close, with the wind and sea both knocking the groynes. The little girl shivered and her eyes stung. It must be the salt in the air. Some way out to sea, her brother was splashing.

"It's like pulling a plaster off," Mummy told her. "The quicker the better."

The girl wrote quickly, but with tomboy things she was slow. Or never started.

"Once there was a girl who made the sea warm up just by smiling at it," said Mummy, and smiled.

"All right!" cried the girl, and ran past her, right down to the shore. The wind almost carried her to the grey lacy edge of sea. She ran in, and her body felt like ice was setting inside. It also seemed to remember that this had happened before, and she had swum until she was loose again, and free. Like Gerda. The Snow Queen couldn't hold her prisoner for ever. She swam, even though it was a kind of panicking.

Pop called after her, "Susie! A whizz on waves too!"

Daddy turned from the water and waved. But she couldn't speak yet because her arms felt so solid and stiff. Maybe they were thrashing after all. Water reared up into her eyes and mouth but she couldn't stop.

"Well done, darling," Mummy told her as she swam alongside, as if it was easy and lovely, even though her face looked dark with purple, like a bruise.

What if she died, because she was thin? Could hearts break with cold as well as love? But Mummy always changed colour in the sea, and then she was herself again, apart from her smooth, flat hair. She was small but strong and very determined.

The girl swam with her, and the waves seemed to shrink as she warmed. Her own hair was wet too now, but the frizz didn't soften. It just bushed out from a towel, crispy as autumn leaves. For now she was swimming. Daddy would be proud that she didn't give up. How long would she have to swim before she was allowed?

"Get Daddy!" shouted her brother.

"Nooooo!" cried Daddy. "High treason!"

The girl laughed, and trod water while she scooped. She hated being splashed but splashing was different.

"How could you?" he asked, looking at her.

"Easily!" she cried, and splashed harder.

Daddy had nearly drowned once, when he was little. It was a short story but beautiful because of the rainbow colours he saw, and the warmth and light soft around him. It made him think of heaven, as if he'd had a glimpse, so now he knew there was nothing to be scared of. The girl didn't like to think of heaven because she didn't want anyone to die however dreamy dying was. She kept splashing instead.

Later, Mummy rubbed her dry in the beach hut and Nana poured hot chocolate. The sun peeped out from the clouds and warmed her winter woolly. Daddy decided to make the biggest castle ever, with a drawbridge and moat.

"Tell us the story," said her brother, as the walls took shape.

"Sue can start it," said Daddy. "But no soldiers please."

"Just a lost mermaid," she said, "and a lonely whale."

"Ah," said Daddy, "the best kind of story!"

"It isn't ready yet," she told them, because stories took time.

Cy

When we lived in Lyndhurst in the New Forest there was a van that used to come around during the summer selling Cherryade. **Mum didn't like us to have fizzy drinks so it seemed like a magical elixir to me.** One day Mum had given me a cardboard box to rest on, and as she baked in the kitchen I picked up the felt tips. When she looked down, she was astonished to see that I'd filled its surface with a Heath Robinson style Cherryade Factory. Her amazement made me proud and happy; I wanted to become an artist who could impress people **in the same way.**

Life in the New Forest was idyllic. Dad was the local policeman, playing cricket on the green and tug o' war at the village fete. I was a cowboy whose colt .45 cap-guns glistened with the curlicue patterns embossed on their silver surface. Wearing another homemade outfit, I became Batman nibbling Union-Jack iced fairy cakes at the Queen's Jubilee. I can still see the summer paddling pools, and the robins pecking cream out of milk bottles in winter when we'd roast chestnuts and crumpets on an open fire. I also recall journeys into the forest with sunlight spilling through the canopy, twigs crackling underfoot, and the wind **rushing through the branches like a whispering choir.** I had two Ladybird books of *Sir Gawain and the Green Knight* and *Robin Hood*, and it seemed to me that I was inside the stories on our walks. Mum would take us to sit on a **drooping** branch we called *Dumbo*. It looked like an elephant's trunk and we rode on it as if we were in the jungle.

The woods also held fear. I imagined stumbling across a gingerbread cottage with its cannibalistic hag or into the **turquoise** forest of thorns pictured on the cover of *Sleeping Beauty*. Once on a walk we came across some wild piglets and suddenly there was a crashing and a squealing as their huge mother charged toward us through the undergrowth. Mum grabbed us by the hands and we ran. The adrenalin rush I experienced then resembles my feelings waiting in the wings before a performance. Part of me seeks out this kind of shock, and the clarity that comes with it.

On another occasion, playing in the road, there was a sudden growl of a car engine. As the other children scattered to the pavement I found myself in the path of an oncoming vehicle. The next thing I knew I was under it. Mum, hearing the shrieks from outside, came running out. She told me later her first thought had been whether she should slip on her sandals. It's strange how the mind works in such situations. When the ambulance arrived I was still lying under the car, but it turned out that I only needed a plaster on my finger!

When we lived at Lyndhurst I was a blond-haired, blue-eyed child, but that changed when we moved to Farnham in Surrey. My hair turned brown and, thanks to constant poring over drawings, my eye began to drift into the middle so I had a squint. I got some bottle-end tortoiseshell NHS glasses **and was constantly going backwards and forwards to the opticians having them mended**. Then, chasing my sister and her friend up some concrete steps on our estate, I smashed out my first adult tooth. Right at the front. I ended up with a replacement silver tooth as well as a temporary eye patch.

I'd changed from an angelic Milky Bar Kid to an ultimate nerd, although to be honest, the new look probably suited the inner self, who even then was obsessed with science fiction, superhero comics and drawing. Of course it picked me out and it wasn't long after I joined the school in Hale, Farnham, that Mooler (Mooler, is in retrospect, a great name for a bully) decided to target me on a daily basis. I used to love *wet playtime* when the dinner ladies dished out the crayons, felt-tips, computer paper and reading books and I could indulge my interests and also impress my peers. In the playground I was prey. Mooler would pursue me with a gang of friends and push me down before sitting on my chest and beating my head against the ground. But one day, in the midst of his joy, a figure rounded the corner. It was my sister. Three years older, and tough, she picked him up by the scruff of his neck and held him against the wall until the blood drained from his face. He never bullied me again.

—— *Leslie* ——

For a long time in childhood I felt, with my *Squeaky Clean* voice, that I'd not really met him or that he wasn't really there. His voice in silence wasn't a voice at all, just the clear-headed feeling of passing through life with nothing to declare, while smiling at the others who'd been stopped and told to go back to where they'd come from. No, not a voice, not a feeling, but a quiet, unassuming walk home from school to take up my place at the kitchen table, eating white bread and jam. Because *Squeaky Clean* didn't make a fuss. Happy as a bird, he nested in a high-up place where he couldn't be seen – although he did have his moments: hidden inclinations and things in pockets, fancy things, treasures lifted from cupboards and drawers, all private, all in the dark.

But mostly he was self-possessed. His clothes were smart, his hair was neat and he smiled when spoken to. If there were smells or stains or unpleasant feelings he didn't want to know. He was the face, the nice one in the snapshot who modelled himself on picture-book heroes and fought to save his country.

To me, he was an actor who did as he pleased, refusing to adapt to anyone else. Was he self-satisfied? Quite possibly. Did he look down on me and others? It seemed so. Was he toadying up? More than likely. Certainly he was a bore, a misfit, a pale-faced boy with his head to one side and a vacant expression as if he wasn't really there.

But that all changed when THE SNAKE caught him unawares.

"You don't know me," said the snake as it slithered up his leg and into his belly.

"I'm the top-C snake," it sang, moving in his mouth.

"But I'm very, very secret as well," it added, squeezing through a keyhole into his head.

And there it slept, only coming out at full moon to shed another skin.

From then on he was *Mr Snaky Clean* dressed in school uniform, but *Little Snaky Clean* on the journeys to see family. *Not-So-Clean* as well, when he stuck to the car seat or held back the wee that wriggled and tickled inside him. Afterwards, when he went to the toilet he cried. Then he ate and grew fat like the old lady who swallowed a fly.

When he woke next morning he'd become *Super Squeaky Clean* and the snake had gone. This time, as *S.S.Clean*, he was the dreamer awaiting a sign. Out there in the dark, his thoughts were perfect. In his head there were ghosts, thinned-out feelings and things he'd left behind; but in his heart he was a star. And the other boys were below him. One word from him was enough to stop them in their tracks. So when they were running or trainspotting or climbing trees he was the Man in the Moon.

"I'm Large, you're Small," he told me, in a dream.

I looked at myself in the mirror.

"Larger than you or your parents. Larger than your house," he continued with his face filling out.

I touched myself where I shouldn't.

"Larger than your thoughts," he said and I felt my insides tingle.

"Come with me," he whispered, standing at the window. I wanted to look away.

"See," he told me, pointing to snow on glass.

My breathing had stopped.

"You'll be perfect," he said. Then he took me in his arms and carried me up with the wind to a cold bare place. There we were, white and see-through and absolutely still. And at last I had met him.

Cy

Sandy Hill Estate was a labyrinth of alleyways with creosoted wooden gates and brick and concrete walls. I would ride around it on my sister's blue tricycle feeling like Theseus. I felt so much freedom in the act of pedalling and even now, in flying dreams I have to pedal my legs in the air in order to elevate myself. At school, after my sister's intervention, I'd found lots of friends. I'm not sure if it was because I was the best artist in the class or if I made them laugh or perhaps, sensing my impracticality, they had an instinctive urge to look after me. I couldn't tie my shoelaces and would forget my lunchbox almost every day, but the children in my class would eagerly run back and get it for me and tie up my laces. I sometimes feel that my comedy partner Sam has looked out for me in the same way.

It was about this time that a kid called Stuart turned up from Tottenham in London. With his black hair and Fonzy leather jacket and brilliant football skills he quickly displaced me as the most interesting kid in class. I hated him and we got into a skirmish or two. However, we soon realised that with my artistic skills and his *coolness* we would work better as a double act. We began writing and performing whole-school puppet shows, illustrating a comic together, and gathering others to play *Star Wars* on the fort-cum-death star in the playground. He was incredulous that I always wanted to play Darth Vader (he, in the leather jacket, of course, was Han Solo).

"But you have to lose if you're the baddie?" he said.

I didn't care. Vader was my role. My mum made me a red lightsabre for my birthday out of a torch, sweet wrappers and a roll of greaseproof paper.

I was sad to say goodbye to Stuart when we moved to Botley, Hampshire – where we lived in a wonderful police house, backing onto a field of horses. My dad's miniature police station, tacked onto the side of the house, was where my friends and I were allowed to try on his helmet and handcuff each other. On the table was a wind-up air raid siren next to a book of instructions in case of a nuclear attack. Once a year he had to test the siren. It echoed down the village lanes with an unnerving banshee-like howl. The book told him to take a brush and a bucket and cycle through the village whitewashing the windows to protect the inhabitants from the flash, as bright as the sun. Like Raymond Briggs' *When the wind blows* it also had instructions on how to build a safe den in which to wait until the danger had passed.

In the Lars Von Triers film *Melancholia* we see Kirsten Dunst's character building a den out of sticks to survive the collision of an oncoming planet. I often think of this as an illustration of the fragility of existence in the face of inevitable destruction. There is something beautiful in the absurdity of it.

Just after we'd moved in, Bill, a gamekeeper, a giant of a man, turned up on our doorstep in a tweed trilby hat with feathers in it, clutching a brace of pheasants as a welcoming gift. He patrolled an area by the river where I remember walking with my mum, at some distance behind my dad and sister. Mum was, as usual, pointing out different berries and plants and wildlife to me. Suddenly from ahead came a scream. It was my sister. Rising alongside came a lower sound, warm and deep but deadly. In slow motion it seemed, my sister came running out of the bushes, chased by a black cloud of glistening eyes. As she drew closer with her mouth stretched wide and bulging eyes, we realised she had stepped in a wasps' nest. I'll never forget Mum picking the buzzing wasps from her knee-length white socks or the terror I felt in that moment. At times of anxiety I still dream of wasps.

Mum had a great imagination. As well as *speckled egg walks* where she'd surreptitiously hide bright coloured candied eggs in makeshift birds' nests for us to discover along a route, she also made a *lollipop tree* out of a branch covered in silver foil on the windowsill. Buds would appear and then small lollies, before they grew into bigger and bigger lollies as time went on. She made our shopping trips into adventures, ending with pick 'n' mix and a reading of *Tom Sawyer and Huckleberry Finn* in the park.

—— ***Leslie*** ——

As a boy, I shared my life with my *Voice Defence*. First up on the show, he put out statements about why I might have done that or what I really meant when I put it that way. As the voice in my ear, he briefed me all day on how to sit properly, talk nicely, and what to do if I dried up. He chose the angle on breaking news, wrote the editorial, and was first to be asked by the people behind the show for updates and commentary on long-running stories. Nothing escaped his eye: my thoughts about my dad, what I'd hidden in my pocket, how old I looked in the mirror and the things I'd missed out on. He called himself my apologist, perhaps too readily, because sometimes it seemed he didn't really mean it. He interrupted often, focusing on my failures, and once he got started wouldn't let go.

Like a Hindu god, my *Voice Defence* came in different versions. On Mondays he wore blue, had money in his pocket and whistled Colonel Bogey as we walked to school.

"Chin up," he said, "you're on the menu, but it's not forever."

For the next three days he wore black and spoke like a priest in mourning.

"Why did you do that?" he'd ask after I'd lost my balance while kicking a ball.

"You should know better," he said when I was sent to the Head's office for talking in class.

"Pretend you're not here," he said when a boy made rude noises and squared up for a fight.

For the rest of the week my *Voice Defence* kept his head down. Left alone, he pulled faces and talked to himself; if disturbed, he was waspish. He was the lazy dog who didn't want to be bothered, and the sleeper in the corner with wolfish thoughts. So he'd huff and puff, play grandma's footsteps, brush his teeth white and gobble you up.

"I'll have you lot for breakfast!" he barked, imitating the teacher.

"You're a doggie-do!" he cried in the playground.

"We're off the lead!" he called at home time.

And his words came in whimpers, snarls, growls, yelps, howls.

At night, in dreams, my *Voice Defence* did things. When the small boys asked questions he got them in his sights and told them to buzz off. When the big boys squared up, he stared them down. Hidden at the back of the classroom he interrupted the teacher with loud coughs, blaming them on me to avoid detention. When his parents spoke he pretended not to hear. He ran through flower beds growling at cats and making ghostie noises. With his blindfold, gag and catapult he took me prisoner and together we laid siege to the house. He was Mr Nobody who blew open the back door and muddied the carpet. And he leaked in the bed, picked his nose, had ink-stained fingers and chewed his nails till he drew blood.

So what about me?

I was the nice boy filling myself up with sweets and lemonade. The boy on his own who played himself at cards or tried his hand at the puzzles he'd collected from cereal packets. The boy with a book in his head – who prayed and smiled and stared into space as he tuned-out the world. But inside that boy was the voice of experience telling him to grow up. No more scaredy-cat or silly-silly. There were people out there who didn't understand: my parents were worried, the teachers were cross and the boys all laughed. Nobody heard me when I asked for a friend, a day off school, or cried in the bath. And when I prayed for help or lay awake listening in bed, or tiptoed to the toilet in the dark – well of course, you've guessed it – my *Voice Defence* wasn't there.

—— *Cy* ——

At Freegrounds Junior School in Botley I resumed my role as *artist in residence*. My teacher Mr Conway let me skip Maths to work on the class display. Both he and I were determined that it was going to be the best.

I was fascinated by a print on my parents' wall of Salvador Dali's *Metamorphosis of Narcissus*. I studied the crowd in the background and the sculpture on a plinth on a chessboard. I puzzled over the road running past some buildings and around a mountain, asking where did it lead? When Mum and Dad explained to me the self-love story behind the picture it brought home, by compari-

son, how far my image was from how I wanted to look. I think this probably accounts for my self portraits over a long period where I either idealised myself or turned myself into a cartoon-like figure inhabiting an imaginary world. After reading *The Voyage of the Dawn Treader* I'd occasionally close my eyes and dip my hand tentatively into our Dali art books in the hope of joining his world, all sadly to no avail. On a trip to London, the surrealism of *Autumnal Cannibalism* mesmerised me, joining my love of dreamscapes from *Alice in Wonderland* to Edward Lear, from Dali to Magritte. Reality and fiction were never far apart. I wrote a semi-autobiographical sketch in which my character *Bern* scrabbled to pass through wardrobes and smashed his teeth out trying to jump into pavement pictures.

Mum and Dad were keen adventurers and bought an orange VW camper van. In our flimsy Peter Storm anoraks and wellington boots we headed off to The Lake District, The Highlands, Dartmoor and The Pennines on walking holidays and these often rain-soaked excursions led to many a first-hand encounter with the brutality of nature. Once, as we crossed Dartmoor, Dad got lost in the mist and Mum decided to take control.

"This way!" she said. "Follow Mummy!"

On saying this she stepped off a tuft of grass and sank almost to her waist in the marsh.

I was horrified. I'd seen *The Hound of the Baskervilles* with Christopher Lee and Peter Cushing, and the image of a hand grasping at the air as someone sank into a bog was burnt into my mind.

Dad, of course, had to drag her out.

On another occasion I'd broken my arm and with it still in a cast and my glasses steamed up, we followed Mum and Dad along a mountain pass with a sheer drop on one side. I felt the panic rise in my chest as I squinted down into the mist on the edge of the precipice. I survived, probably more by good luck than judgement, but it did help me to relate to *The Lost World* or *Journey to the Centre of the Earth* on a more realistic level.

I spent a good deal of my free time not only reading, but writing and drawing. Both focused on the adventures of a solitary figure called *Snod* pitting his wits against an absurd world.

He was the first of my fictional alter egos, based on Don Quixote amalgamated with Dali and my love of all things Spanish. Mum and Dad often played Rodriguez's *Concierto de Aranjuez* and it was to this soundtrack that my character travelled across the plains of Andalusia, which I saw also as a sheet of white paper stretching to the edge of my imagination that I wanted to fill with unknown cities and characters.

―― *Leslie* ――

The voice of the poet wasn't like mine. Although we were friends, I was a child and the poet was much older.

"It's a dream," the poet said as we stepped out to the back garden.

The birds flew up. Their wings made the sound of dresses, rustling.

"Another country," the poet said as we walked up the path.

The worms came out. Their bodies were jam doughnuts sliced on a plate.

"In here," the poet whispered as we hid in the shed.

The rain tap-danced on the roof.

"See these," said the poet, turning out dusty tools from a box.

The wind blew sand in our faces.

"Outside now."

And the orchestra began. A child called out; a blackbird sang; bees hummed the tune.

When we walked into the runner bean patch, the poles made a church. Looking up, we named them: flowers in stone, leaves as tracery, bean pod gargoyles.

The steps behind were Stations of the Cross.

When we climbed to the bank, the spiders were there, watching. Their webs were drawstrings on old grey bags.

Later, the poet took me on a tour. The street we walked along seemed like a border crossing. It led behind houses to an abandoned track. Our path looked out over wide open fields where everything was strange, yet oddly familiar. Passing through time zones we stopped by a wall, a nettle patch, a dried-out pool. Turning through a gate, the trees closed in. The wood we'd entered was a land full of light and shade and living material. Things we couldn't see followed us at a distance, moving tree to tree. They were the ghosts of poets whose words filled our heads.

Later still, I made up my mind to become the poet. So I wrote lines to him and about him and read them back silently; I stared hard into the mirror, hoping to discover my true self; I stood at the window and grew imaginary wings. I was on a high, aware of the gap but ready to do anything – and I willed myself on like a pumped-up runner.

The poet wasn't having any of it.

"You can't force a poem," the poet said.

In the quiet back garden the shadows on the lawn were lengthening.

"And it's not yours to have," said the poet.

The houses on the street were beginning to blur.

"A poem is a poem is a poem," the poet said.

Fine rain had spread across the fields.

"There's nothing more to say," the poet said, leaving. When I followed him outside, the street was empty and the sky was a blank sheet of paper.

The poet died and became a star. It was winter, and the earth was cold. At the funeral, the poet's ashes were hailstones on grass. In the street, the doorbells were silent. Birds in the fields flew up and away. Afterwards, when I sat in the garden I looked up, but the sky was colourless. The star had fallen and passed into stone. The words that filled my mind were ice dropped in water.

When spring arrived I walked in the woods. As the leaves returned I felt the poet in me. Stepping through softness I searched for memories. Sunlight fell on roots and branches; new shoots and birdsong filled the air; one by one the bulbs unfolded. I was alone in a world full of colour and brightness. And I wrote.

Cy

It was while hiking with Mum and Dad in the Julian Alps that I first discovered the magic properties of drink. After a long, dry, hungry, exhausting climb on *Matajur*, a huge goatherd had appeared in the doorway of a small cottage, gesturing to us with two enormous brown hands. Dressed in wool and leather, he had a large moustache and a bulbous red nose. Peering over this were two sparkling eyes, like buttons sewn into weathered brown skin. He ushered us into his small dark hut, which smelt of goat and unwashed man. While we perched on wooden milking stools he fumbled excitedly around, producing a bottle of Slivovice and a leather beaker. My Dad, realising that the man hadn't seen anyone for a long time, indicated that we shouldn't refuse the toast. I remember the taste of it, hot and sweet, burning my throat slightly on the way down. But as his warm, deep, friendly voice talked to us in his own tongue, sprinkled with a dash of pidgin English, I began to feel the ache in my limbs disappear and my spirits lift. Slivovice, I decided, was a magical potion. The goatherd shook our hands and gave us a message for his wife in the town below, who he hadn't seen for year. It was a wonderful encounter. My sister and I bounded up the mountainside afterwards feeling invincible.

Our travels with Mum and Dad also taught us about respecting nature. We'd bathe naked in icy mountain pools and then discover a dead sheep lying in the stream that fed it further up the pass. Once, in a lonely Pyrenean valley, while I watched my parents climb to the snow line, about a thousand sheep and a huge mountain dog had streamed down a slope towards me. Mum and Dad saw through binoculars the look of fear in my face as a shepherd approached me. He was surprised to see me, but very warm and friendly.

In the mountains one feels isolated and small, like looking out into space, but also utterly real. It's at once frightening yet exhilarating, and although at the time I'm sure I cursed both my parents as I struggled on these pilgrimages, I thank them for the gift of solitude and silence I received on these epic walks.

Sue

Bonfire Night made winter exciting, but safe and small. The girl would hate a crowd with fatty smells, and a sack man, as human as a scarecrow, burning on a fire – losing his face, his body melting like cheese. And people enjoying it! Had she seen that once? Because the picture was red and cruel and flaring in her head, and came with smoke that choked. If only the story wasn't full of gunpowder and torture. She'd seen the Rack at the Tower of London with Daddy and it was too evil to believe in. She might hate History if it wasn't so long ago it was hardly real – like being a baby in a washing-up bowl staring at Daddy as if nothing meant anything.

At home there was no Guy, just fireworks Daddy lit outside in the cold, while they stayed indoors with tomato soup, and toast speared and browned on a smaller fire, the one Daddy had to make up with coal each morning. With the curtains pulled open the living room was like a stage and they were in the front row of the stalls. Through the wall of glass, behind their silly-faced reflections, was blackness – and in it Daddy was being careful, crouching with matches and blue touch-paper. All they had to do was watch and wait for the next surprise. Each one was starry and beautiful, and fizzed or spun or lifted off beyond the trees.

"Rocket!" her brother cried hopefully each time. His socks were flopping off but that made them better for sliding.

The waiting was part of the show, with a mouth full of hot food, and hot chocolate in a mug. And every time the silence ended with quiet colour, the two of them jumped inside, or pretended to. Every time the last sparks were lost in the darkness, it was like the last lick of a Mr Whippy.

But when the dangerous part was over and Daddy beckoned, they put on coats and hats, scarves and mittens, and wellies for speed. That meant sparklers for lighting up faces, snatches of washing line, border or path. For threading a message in silver script that soon became a mystery – so it was really a secret, like a *Man from U.N.C.L.E.* code. And the red heat on the stick glared as it sent the sparks off in showers, making it hard not to forget the adverts about children blinded and rushed screaming to hospital. So it felt just slightly brave. Not that it was as risky as Mummy at her age, tightrope walking the narrow wall over the railway bridge for a dare. The girl knew she didn't have that kind of bravery, and didn't want it either. She liked the sound of sparklers, so soft it was like a private conversation. She liked the once-a-year smell left behind when they went back inside to warm up before bed with a book Daddy might read them, if he wasn't too tired.

―― *Leslie* ――

I spent the day after Bonfire Night collecting burnt-out fireworks. One by one I picked up their hollow-out casings and stored them in a cardboard box. They were all shapes and sizes. Some were shredded or had fused into lumps, while others were hollowed out. Their insides were coated with what looked like coal dust.

When I'd collected my fireworks I lined them up on the path, making whooshing and popping noises and calling out warnings to spectators as I moved down the line with an imaginary lighter. Some of them sparked straight away and some fizzled out. A rocket launched itself several times, some jumping crackers kept banging and popping at random intervals, while my sparklers just went on and on. It was my smoke-and-mirrors show where I alone witnessed what others couldn't see.

Around that time I was going through my counting and collection phase. Counting steps while looking out for coins, collecting sticks and stones, retrieving pegs and bottle tops from grass – I was the jackdaw-boy taking my finds and hiding them in corners. Later, I'd return and dig up my hoards; or if I didn't survive, they would tell my story.

Fireworks were dangerous. I'd been told that so often that the phrase had lost its meaning. In my world they were fountains, jumping jacks, candles, starbursts. So fireworks were an adventure, a big bang show similar to circus – only fireworks were more graceful, like flowers in the air. For me each burst was a lift and an *ah*. They went up with a whoosh and scattered like seeds. And when they fell back to earth they were hollowed out like shells on a beach.

Looking back, I see my childhood games as an attempt to placate the powers that be – as my dad called them. Everything was in the hands of a Searchlight God, someone up there overhearing my bad thoughts and marking me for punishment. So I quickly backtracked and unsaid things, promising to reform. I counted my steps and held my breath as I asked for forgiveness. I was the runaway playing *catch-me* as I ducked for cover behind walls. And all my actions were directed by fear and superstitious reverence.

My firework display was a one-day wonder. After lining them up and firing them at intervals, I returned them to their box. Seeing their colours and after-image flashes had kept me in that world where anything was possible. It had fed my dreams, played out daily, where I ran my own life. Fireworks were like thoughts: they sparked at anything. Once a year they took over gardens and lit up the rooftops. They were always there, flashing warnings from corners in the dark.

One day, like them, I'd explode.

—— Cy ——

Going up to secondary school introduced me to a far wider group of friends (including some whose parents had been arrested by my dad). We discovered *Dungeons and Dragons* together, followed by *The Young Ones* and *Red Dwarf* on television. I was cheeky and for the most part confident and everyone seemed to accept the fact that I was slightly odd. I moved comfortably between smoking cigarettes with the Stony Lane group and the nerdy crowd. Comedy and a sense of anarchy were probably my saving grace. From dressing up the skeleton in the Science room as the teacher and hiding behind it mimicking her voice, to staff caricatures scrawled on my exercise books, I never took things too seriously. My English teacher, Mr Hammond, encouraged my rebellious streak, writing "Spot on Cy!" under a picture of him being attacked by a group of punks with catapults and, "I don't know whether to give you an E or an A," under my long satirical answers to literary questions.

During the first few secondary school years my friend Luke and I came up with the concept of a fictional band – originally inspired by Douglas Adams' *Restaurant at the end of the Universe*. We called them *Vomit*. I wrote the lyrics and Luke, who could play by ear, recreated my hummed tunes using his bedroom equipment. We roped in Ivan who was a guitarist and put together our first album – *Freak Out and Throw Up*. It was originally just an intellectual exercise but soon I managed to convince them both that we should perform it on stage to the whole school. Admittedly the title track, *I love your glands* ("let me rip 'em out your body and I'll squeeze 'em in my hands.") was probably not brilliant musically with its plodding baseline, screeching synth guitars and us shouting over the top, but I remember it being greeted enthusiastically and kids spending their dinner money on buying the audio tape of the album afterwards. Other songs included a Noel Cowardesque acapella love song to a terrapin that I actually performed again only last year. I have never stopped writing and performing comedy songs, from Sam and Cy's *The Clap* and *Georgie the Chicken* songs to recent collaborations with Al and the brilliant Lobby Lud including the very catchy *Fungi Forage*.

The pinnacle of Vomit's life came with our final leaving-school performance and the second album *Under the Waves*. It took shape in Luke's bedroom, full of all sorts of technological wizardry, with me watching in awe as his fictional rock star image lifted from the page and he began to inhabit it completely. With his jet-black hair, pallid complexion, purple-lined cape, eyeliner and silver-topped cane he was the epitome of Goth. Not only did we write the songs together but Luke also introduced me to Baudelaire and HP Lovecraft, The Sisters of Mercy and Jesus and Mary Chain. He refused to eat or drink anything without the word black in it – black coffee, black cherry yoghurt – and we laughed about his romantic vision of committing suicide by being struck by lightning at the top of a mountain. We imagined him up there with a ten-foot aerial on his head: an idea I later used in a comedy pilot.

I remember two later meetings vividly. One was sighting Luke on the opposite side of Southampton High Street, walking against the flow of pedestrians with his long black hair and his cape blowing behind him and his cane tapping in front of him. He seemed to stride through the crowd like some beautiful ghost from another realm. Another time I was walking with him and as we passed the park, a hangout for Goths and punks, a group of Goth-girls ran out, surrounding him like a celebrity. "Oh Lucian, Lucian!" they cooed. He looked at me daring me to break his cover, and as we rounded the corner we both burst out laughing.

"Lucian?!"

"I told them my name was Lucian Velvet."

I thought then that he had achieved near-mythical status.

Much later, my great friend Neil told me a story he'd heard from the punks he used to hang out with. One day while Luke was in the park the punks thought it would be funny to pour lighter fuel over *Lucian* and set fire to him. Neil said he didn't even flinch, just stood there in flames staring at them.

"You laughed while I burned," he said and walked, head upright, cane clacking, slowly out of the park in flames.

Neil said it terrified them.

For the final Vomit concert Luke was dressed in full Gothic regalia while Ivan and I wore Hawaiian shorts with flashing builders' lamps in our crotches. The words, taken from Byron, for our parting song were, "Mad, bad and dangerous to know."

By secondary school my favourite subject had become Drama. I was the youngest student to get a role in *Bugsy Malone*, and although I had practised the monologues for weeks before the audition in my finest Brooklyn accent intending to get the lead, I had to settle for the comic-relief character, Knuckles. Mr Hallman, my drama teacher, told me many years later that he cast me as Knuckles because of my talent for comedy. Encouraged by Mr Hallman I went on to take A Level Drama at college, developing more self-confidence. From Alfie to Archie Rice in *The Entertainer* I was always happy to play the lead roles and was a regular on *Whose line is it anyway* at lunchtimes. There were many colourful characters at college, including *hippy* Jim in his tank-top, wide collars and flares and of course Luke (or Lucian) who often resembled a slightly decayed Mr Rochestercum-Chattertonesque suicidal bohemian poet who would swoop into college on bat wings and melt into the shadows in between lectures.

Sue

It might be the fifteenth time but it's always the best because they're together, just the two of them. She holds Daddy's hand and he leads, knowing London, used to trains. On the underground platform she can't help looking on the black track for tails, whiskers; she hasn't forgotten the Hammer Horror rat cornered in his tool shed. But the train rattles in, pushing the air ahead of it and she tries not to think of crushed fur, of bone and blood.

At Leicester Square they surface to smells that never fill Mummy's kitchen, and people from countries she can't always name. She's good, though, at identifying the artists in Daddy's books when he covers the text on the left hand page. Not just Van Gogh, who's easy, but the ones who are long, and hard to spell and pronounce: Meindert Hobbema, Wouwerman, Hieronymus Bosch. She loves it when Daddy's face opens wide in a smile of astonishment and he cries, "I can't catch you out!" as if he's determined to, when really he's glad that she makes it so hard.

At the National Gallery it's not a quiz. It's just happiness. There's a magic, painted box called a Peepshow and when she was little that had to be the first stop, looking through, as if it was a theatre, or a bit like *The Borrowers*. Now she'll be taking the Eleven Plus soon, so she feels grown-up because she knows what's round each corner, centuries, schools. There are her favourites, and Daddy has his too, so when they reach those they always sit on one of the long benches in the middle of the room and look. Really look. Mostly they don't speak much because it's like church, only what you respect is a different kind of greatness. She loves

Murillo's *The Two Trinities* because Mary's face shines and her creamy hand is so gentle and beautiful. But the hands of Rembrandt's old lady are brown and knotty, and more alive. Daddy loves Rembrandt but the darkness is too dingy for the girl. She likes Italian blues, greens and reds – but it doesn't seem possible that Raphael's gorgeously wrapped St Catherine is about to die, on a wheel. Some of the stories are the cruel ones she really doesn't want to know, and she isn't very interested in the big, showy paintings full of important people. But Daddy points out funny things – like the way the monkey's bottom could be the stone ball at the end of the wall, or the stone ball could be the monkey's bottom. You just can't tell, and that's unbelievable because it's like a mistake, and the artist – that was Veronese – would be so upset if he knew they enjoyed the same joke every time.

It's special when the faces seem real because they're lit up inside. Daddy always stops by Gainsborough's *Daughters Chasing a Butterfly* because one of the girls is like that. It's the one Gainsborough loved more; you can see. That's sad for her sister, though, and she must have seen and known when he showed them both the painting. He didn't even finish her properly. The first time Daddy talked about it the girl was a bit jealous, because she didn't think she had that brightness shining through, but now she wonders whether Daddy looks emotional like that because she's his daughter and he loves her anyway. Maybe she has a light only he can see?

Moving on, they find the Avercamp snow scene that's like a cartoon, full of action that's frozen like the ice. It's a bit rude in places but she's not meant to notice. It's so busy, like under the stone where the snakes live. But it's more of a story all the same – one that would take ages to tell because there are so many characters and she doesn't know enough Dutch names. She likes the tiny details more, though, than the naked goddesses who are actually quite fat, fatter than she ever wants to be. Soon she tells Daddy she's starting to like the Impressionists best. Van Gogh's chair makes him seem very lonely. He must have been sad like Daddy can be. She wonders whether he ever had a girl to link arms with through the street, a girl who looked up to him more than anyone.

Pictures are for imagining really, because you never really know what the people are thinking or why. But in *Rain, Steam and Speed* there aren't any people – just a bridge and a train you can hardly see and a rabbit she would never have spotted and most people never notice because they haven't got Daddy to point it out. This art is wild and different, and Turner took a risk which makes it exciting. Inside the carriages, though, there must really be people with stories that started before the journey and the storm, stories that will go on after the sun comes out – unless there's a crash and they all die! She imagines the way Turner would have painted heads and arms lost in angry water, just strokes of paint, no light inside.

Soon it's time for fish and chips and a Knickerbocker Glory at the Quality Inn in Leicester Square. The ice cream comes in such a long glass that there's a special spoon to reach down where the chocolate sauce makes a thick little pool. This is the only restaurant she's ever been to and even though they only come once every eight weeks or so, it's theirs. Not Mummy's or her brother's. Sometimes Daddy says, smiling, "Why not have something different?" but that would be like not stopping at the giant leaping horse called Whistlejacket to stare at the silkiness of his coat, or not wondering whether Mr and Mrs Andrews ever kissed and how Gainsborough mixed that blue that was almost like air.

Daddy pays and takes her hand.

"Thank you," she says.

— *Cy* —

I studied Creative Arts at university. As a relatively new subject, it taught us how the four elements that make up a performance – words, visuals, movement and music – can be used to create meaning. It often seemed to lead to people being suspended upside down and naked, possibly painted blue and screaming in a space that usually contained a fuzzy television screen. The accompanying soundtrack of TV static and the smashing of various instruments with a jackhammer only added to the discomfort and confusion of the freshers, of which I was one. I'd actually wanted to study Fine Art, but my results weren't good enough, thanks to my partying – and the drinking went on. I remember turning in a smashed sherry bottle stuck back together with Elastoplast entitled *Plastered* as one of my art projects.

The problem in halls of residence was that someone, somewhere was always asking me to go drinking or to a party. Ron *The psycho dwarf* lived in the room opposite. His end of the night showpiece was to down the slop bucket in the middle of the dance floor. He'd stand there in his leather biker's jacket and oil-stained jeans pouring the orange bucket into his tiny frame with it cascading out the sides into his long hair. Sometimes I would find him clinging to the wall as if on the edge of a giant seesaw, fishing in his pocket for his key, and once he had it firmly in his hand he would dive for the lock and twist the handle, falling into his room in one deft, drunken movement. Ron was a little like a hairy stuntman for one of the dwarves in *Lord of the Rings*. He spoke in a thick Brummy accent, told me he was a *Hells Angel prospect* and kept a motorcycle engine under his bed. I remember my surprise at seeing him in a suit and tie looking like a miniature Lemmy on his way to a court hearing and him telling me he was teaching his first class at a local school. We used to sit in his room smoking pot and listening to Tom Waits' deep, croaky tales of smoky bars and broken hearts, prostitutes and drunks.

I can't recall how I met Neil, only his blue manic stare. It was strange because he'd grown up in Southampton close to me and we had a lot of friends in common. We even worked out we'd been to the same parties, just never met, or never remembered we'd met. We shared a love of Ska and were often found jogging on the spot along to The Specials. We'd both been reading *Zen and the Art of Motorcycle Maintenance* which led to discussions on the nature of reality and an attempt to read Immanuel Kant's *Critique of Pure Reason*. When we met to discuss our progress over a bottle of Midori Melon liqueur, neither of us had got far past the first page and so we decided to write a limerick instead.

We drank a bottle of Midori,
While discussing a priori,
We got very pissed
And said I exist
And that's the end of the story.

Neil introduced me to Kurt Vonnegut and the Bonzo Dog Doo-dah band. We quickly formed an artistic double act called *Snod and Ichabod*, writing surreal articles for the college magazine, dropping acid and making films together. We also laughed an awful lot. For my honours project I made a film called *Exit* with Neil playing the central character *Derelict Winch* – a man who strives to be real but finds everything he does turns into a fictional scenario. While out walking he would hear an orchestra start up and have a compulsion to sing as if in a musical; if popping down to the shops he would find himself in the middle of a shootout followed by a car chase. Neil was a great actor and played it completely straight. I'd gone about the process of putting together my film in complete seriousness but as we sat back to watch the first edited sequence I heard a squeak and then a snort beside me. I looked at Neil and realised his face was bright red.

"I ... I'm sorry," he said.

"It's funny isn't it?" I asked.

"Hilarious," he replied.

We watched it back again, this time both crying with laughter. I had to accept that my high-art film had turned into comedy.

It played to packed houses full of laughter. One student said it *was the best thing I've seen at this uni*. The problem was that everyone was trying to produce something thought-provoking and avant-garde and often pieces turned out humourless. In breaking the mould, mine was closer to accidental anarchy, something I seemed quite skilled at. I remember nailing a crucified Mickey Mouse to a large fluorescent orange cross and carrying him from halls to the performance space. I found myself caught up in a crowd and forced to the front with my artwork held high like a placard. When I emerged next to the reception area, there was Princess Anne and me, the lone protestor. What exactly the protest was about wasn't clear but it was certainly something the protestor believed in strongly judging by the amount of work he'd put into that placard.

My house share at university with Sam began by me walking in on him and Paul dancing barefooted to the song *Barefootin'* in our front room. Paul directed Sam and me in our first routine called *Hat*. It sprang from a conversation with Sam about my new woolly hat, which Paul turned into a sketch. He'd realised that there was something intrinsically funny about our interactions.

A few years later, when Paul and I came across a bottle of white *Bikini Rum* that tasted like paint-stripper, we spent the evening inventing a 50's style ad campaign for it with the tag-line "Guess who's been drinking Bikini?" We imagined a billboard showing a poolside party at a mansion in Beverly Hills with various bathing beauties and musclemen laughing as they sip cocktails. Behind them, a bottle of Bikini lies empty on its side and two feet are sticking up from behind a garden table where someone has collapsed. As in *Hat*, our best scripts were often wild adaptations from life.

DEVELOPING AN ACT

— *Cy* —

I remember waiting back stage at the first *Sam and Cy* gig after returning from Edinburgh and wondering where my nerves had gone. I felt supremely confident, like a master of my art. When we first started performing in variety shows at the Brentwood Theatre I'd often vomit and see myself running away seconds before stepping onto the stage. We used to come on to *Thus Spake Zarathustra* by Strauss, both as a homage to and spoof of Elvis's Las Vegas stage shows. It was a huge build-up and I would feel my heart pounding in my chest and the nausea rising as the music reached its climax. We entered wearing Royal Variety-style dress shirts and bow ties, but in reality our material sprang from the boredom of household chores in our shared house at university. While Sam was hoovering I would hide in a wardrobe like Kato in the Peter Sellers Pink Panther films and leap out on him with a karate chop. Sam would often do the same and we'd fly into combat springing out from under duvets or softly padding up, cat-like, to surprise each other while washing the dishes. The battles were never finely choreographed and after an initial chop and kick we'd often have to resort to what we'd learnt in playground scuffles: the Chinese burn, the pinch, the nose twist. The strange noises we made were based on the sounds we'd heard dubbed onto martial arts fights in the 70s – a bit of Monkey Magic with a sprinkle of the Kung Fu TV Series with David Carradine. It was very silly as an opening, but people laughed and once we were on stage we enjoyed it.

At home, the script was the same.

"So, we meet again my old friend."

"Indeed we do – but this time the advantage is mine you see, this is not my true identity."

"That is not your true identity? Then reveal yourself to me!"

We would then pretend to pull off layer after layer of rubber masks á la *Mission Impossible*. Each character beneath was built up through improvisations in which we would try to outdo each other by revealing yet another twist to the story.

"That is where you are mistaken you see – I AM your Auntie," or: "I was hoping you'd finally admit the truth you see I AM you!"

Our favourite sequence, and one that always made us laugh, went from the milkman to a school teacher in the Scottish Highlands through a series of rapid character changes ending with Sam and me performing our own opera.

—— *Sue* ——

The hall fills up with older girls but she's not really nervous. She's in costume, and the lines she wrote are stored in her head like Wordsworth's *Daffodils*. When she wrote the script she always knew she'd be Francis Drake so maybe it's good that her chest is flat inside the homemade doublet. Even though she's seen Errol Flynn out

fence the Sheriff enough times, she's not sure how dashing she can be. But she'll try.

Daddy said he was proud and astonished but he can't be here. Neither can Mummy, who's helped with scrap materials even though she stitches by hand and the other mums have machines. Queen Elizabeth's cardboard ruff is standing up well but can't be comfy. The girl didn't imagine what the older girls might see, think or mutter. She's eleven and a half and most of them are teenagers. It wasn't her idea to invite them, or even perform the play instead of just having fun with it at lunchtimes, but once someone told the teachers, they used the word *talent* and she liked it. She thought she could carry that feeling onto the stage. It might help her look at the clock at the back of the hall and not mind her legs or her hair.

She's excited; it's a kind of bravery. But she can tell some of her friends are wondering what she's got them into. It's her show and her fault. There's a prompt ready with her script just in case she has to whisper a cue. The audience members have their illustrated programmes. The music starts. The last few girls take their seats. It's serious now, like it was for Shakespeare. The curtain will soon go up. And she's in the first scene, and every other. Does that make her a show-off, the kind Mummy can't stand? A bighead? Isn't it just like playing for the first eleven?

She can act in front of the mirror and she's heard that famous people are shy, like Hancock and Cher. There's no choice now anyway and it's better than being a courtier in Cinderella with no name and no lines, and this time there won't be any photos.

—— *Cy* ——

In our first London show at The King's Head Theatre we had woven our mask-removing act into an hour-long show with sword fighters, secret agents, our two Lancashire Pensioners Edie and Len (of whom I think Sam and I were both immensely fond), Crocodile Dundee-style Australian survival experts and many more. It was like a wild, brightly coloured comic book adventure and after we'd performed a part of it on stage at the Cambridge Comedy Festival the compère described us as *the hardest working men in comedy*. It was frenetic; there was an innocent joy in it and we'd often discussed how it was therapy. Removing masks was Jungian but it also looked back to Greek Theatre. Being two connected us with the Janus mask, with comedy and tragedy, The Twins, and one's own shadow. As combatants we became figures haunted by forgotten people or objects and dark, repressed memories. There was the exploration of identity and of course there was a nod to Commedia dell'arte in the stock characters and farcical scenarios. I remember once we actually put together an opening sequence to a show with our director Paul Battin where we all played each other and various members of Sam's family who were in the audience! Sam had struggled with some aspects of living back at home and had poured his thoughts and frustrations into the sketch. We would often take on the guise of each other's parents or at times jilted lovers or betrayed friends. We had great fun doing it and it always felt like a beautiful cleansing of oneself.

What we'd really done was to put our friendship on stage. From being 18 year old freshers sharing a tiny room with bunk beds adjacent to the halls of residence toilets, we had shared an ability to laugh at the absurdity of real life and at one another. We laughed at our narcissism, our naivety, and the habits and idiosyncrasies that made us who we were. We laughed at our fears and helped each other to escape into a surrealist world of invented characters and scenarios. Once, we overheard the boyfriend of a good friend saying, "Who do they think they are? Laurel and fucking Hardy?"

Years later, on the drive back from a Manchester gig, we pretended to be pensioners Edie and Len – mad as it may sound we wrote a lot of material on those road trips! But Sam was feeling tired and decided it would be best to pull over in a service station to have a nap. He'd put some sleeping bags in the back of the car and so he drove over to a quiet, dark corner of the car park and we wound the seats back and snuggled down. Shortly afterwards there was a rapping at the window. We both turned and were lit up by the torchlight of a policeman peering into the car. Instantly, we knew what he was thinking and got the giggles. He signalled to wind the window down. I can't remember but I'm guessing he said something akin to *evening gentlemen*. Certainly that's the kind of thing policemen often say in fiction and although this was a real policeman he has now become fictionalised in the telling of this story.

Of course Sam and I knew this wasn't the best scenario to be sniggering at. We were also aware that the policeman probably thought we were involved in some nefarious shenanigans and the explanation would inevitably involve us saying we were comedians. We both imagined him shouting to an unseen colleague "Oy, Jim, looks like we've got a couple of comedians here!"

—— Sue ——

Things the girl hated at fourteen:
Her hair.
Nana paying for her hair to be shampooed and set at the old ladies' salon, where the hairdryer burned her ears.
Her hair coming out straighter, but stiff.
Having to wear a rain hat on her bike after that, to stop her hair breaking out again.
Cycling to school with girls who were thinner, prettier and faster.
Being fat.
Having less pocket money than anyone she knew.
The way Mum talked to strangers on trains and in the street.
The way Mum knew everyone in town and they all said the girl looked exactly like her.
The make-up ban.
Having no period yet, and no breasts, which made her practically a freak.
Blushing.
What boys thought of her.
Being Div.4 for Maths, and the French teacher telling everyone in the top set that she was *incredulous* about that.
Hockey, especially in mud – and worst of all, in goal where that ball was scary.
Being the last one left on the bench in the cloakroom when captains were picking their teams.
Dogs, especially if they jumped and barked.
Sand between her toes.
Dad's work, because sometimes on Sundays he couldn't bear the thought of the week to come.
Things the girl loved at fourteen:
Going by train to London with Dad, for art, ballet, Shakespeare or a film, and lunch in a restaurant.

Walking with Dad on Sundays.
English.
Coming top in English.
Jesus, especially at Easter.
Sydney Carton, JFK and Atticus Finch.
All the actors and lead singers penned along her ruler.
Her brother being funny. Beating him now and then at ping pong and garden golf.
Mum's macaroni cheese, ice cream with a 99 Flake, Walnut Whip.
Riding her bike in the countryside when it was sunny but not too hot.
Writing poems, and showing them to Dad.
Reading – especially in the garden, with Dad in the next deck chair.
Roses, orange blossom and jasmine.
The sound of the sea.
Dancing when no one saw.

—— *Cy* ——

Our *Sam and Cy* residency at The Canal Cafe Theatre was an exciting time. We'd been signed up by an agent to perfect an Edinburgh show by replacing the characters and sketches that weren't working with new material until we had developed something tight and funny. We were enthused. We flyered around London and expected that we would be performing to a packed house in what was a great venue for us. There was nobody there. Not one audience member. London is a huge place with lots of exciting things going on, and without publicity why would anyone waste good money on coming to see complete unknowns? Any self-respecting comedian probably would have gathered an audience of family and friends for an opening night, but we wanted a *real* audience and had naively thought our success at The King's Head, flyers, and a small listing in *Time Out* would bring them to see us on a Wednesday night. We didn't give up though. The next Wednesday brought an audience of two; undeterred we performed the full hour. One of them turned out to be a journalist, which was promising. We got a bigger piece in *Time Out* and finally slightly larger audiences began to turn up. Craig Charles of *Red Dwarf*, with whom we shared an agent, came along as did the people from the Pleasance Edinburgh who agreed to give us a slot in the Pleasance Attic in 2001.

The show felt strong. New characters included Frank and Bern (his psychopathic brother), a character I still write for and play today. Originally based on some quotes from an article on Charles Bronson I'd seen in the paper, Bern took on a life of his own. He's such an unlikely caricature of a man, but I've met many different versions of him down the years that have informed his evolution. We had the psychiatrist sketch in which my malevolent psychiatrist tries to drive Sam mad through his mind games. I'd been writing psychiatrist sketches since I was 15 with this character in mind so he came quite fully formed with the addition of an Edinburgh accent – in retrospect quite brave to take to the fringe!

Sue

"It's about personality," the judges said, just the way they did on Miss World. The girl didn't really believe them but she wanted to. Or she wanted not to care whether they meant it, because beauty didn't matter and contests were silly anyway. If it was lunchtime fun, like *Just a Minute* and *Call my Bluff*, then they could call it *a laugh* and not care. The three friends agreed, so she took in a dress, her favourite. But the first round was in uniform. She wore stupid stockings with annoying suspenders instead of long brown socks, and brushed her hair extra-hard in the cloakroom. She'd stand out in the crowd as usual anyway.

They were given three consecutive numbers as they waited to circle the hall. She saw that it was mostly first and second years; the big-busted upper school girls who acted in plays had stayed away. Watching, the three friends joked in whispers about being bound to be first, second and third. Then they began their circuit. Remembering that she hadn't earned her Posture Stripe yet, which made her behind the rest with that as well as *the curse*, the girl tried to straighten her back and lift her neck. That would help anyway; her face was too round. Her nose was too piggy. Her legs were too thick. Now her cheeks reddened as she walked, and she wondered why the three of them had decided they "might as well" when they might have chosen outside, a club, or spectating. But Dougi had long, smooth hair, and Pea's large eyes were dark brown. One of the many other Susans could be a model and had a lovely smile with perfect teeth. There were girls with glossy hair, busts, waists ... and she was still a lump. Just a lump with a lot of Honour Marks.

The music stopped. She willed a miracle like Paul Gallico's in the story with the donkey that Dad used to read her. One of the teachers called out a few numbers. Not theirs. The other Susan smiled at the sound of hers and the three friends smiled at her as they made their way out. The girl hoped she'd win.

It was hard to remember posture because she was giggling. It was like the three of them being bottom, second and third bottom in the Gym exam, like having to be in goal and jumping out of the ball's way to let it in, or getting C Minus in Maths when she was supposed to be clever: hopeless, useless, rubbish. It was clowning. That was why they'd entered, to make a joke of it. Thrown out in the first round! It was nearly as funny as when teachers mentioned human reproduction or brassieres.

Inside there was a different story but that was not for telling.

—— Cy ——

There are times outside time. Moments that seem to exist at the beginning and end of everything, like a point on a circle. I've experienced many of these with some beautiful people, none more so than Sam, and there is one in particular that is still going on somewhere.

It was a warm summer's night at the house we all shared after University: Sam Ball, Paul Battin our director, Leigh another friend and writer, and myself. The stars flecked the sky and Sam and I were stood beneath a tree in the garden. To me it felt like *Waiting for Godot*.

I'd been re-reading *One Flew over the Cuckoo's Nest* alongside The *Electric Kool Aid Acid Test*. It seemed to me that there was very little divide between ourselves and our patients on the wards of the psychiatric hospital and I remember enthusiastically eulogising at length about psychosis and the distinctions between sanity and madness. What I hadn't seen was that Sam had had enough. It was over. Not just the party, for the time being, but *Sam and Cy*. This wouldn't be the first time, what I later referred to as, my *Straitjacket* side took control. Someone once called it "Yc" the opposite of "Cy" – the other me.

It would be two years before the second half of the *Sam and Cy* story began.

The notebook I kept is a testament to my lifestyle at the time and my state of mind. It leaps from kaleidoscopic exuberance to deep melancholy and the peaks and troughs of my wildly shifting moods are plainly visible in the artwork and phrases that cover its pages.

— *Sue* —

Her two best friends thought she was funny – or zany, like The Monkees. And with them, that was what she was free to be. They just protested when she sang *He Ain't Heavy, He's My Brother* on the corridor between lessons, but that was a kind of game. The secret rule was that when they groaned, she upped her volume. She was unstoppable. Only she wasn't sure how bad her voice really sounded; it was fine in her head, with the electric guitar and keyboards, and she knew all the words of all the songs in the chart. Every Sunday evening she listened to *Pick of the Pops* with Alan Freeman and wrote down the top twenty, with arrows up or down, in her best handwriting. On Mondays that list drew a crowd before registration and that was something to look forward to.

The three of them had other friends and were part of a crowd made up of girls who didn't swear, thought smoking was horrible and wore sensible shoes with no heel. But mostly, for meeting up outside school and phone calls at weekends, they were a trio. It helped that the other two weren't slim. They liked the same books, music, films and TV shows, but they didn't love anything or anyone as much as she did. All three of them had nicknames provided by the other two – or, in the girl's case, by the Geography teacher who had thrown a chalk at her with the cry, "Let's wake up Shampton at the back." He missed and everyone laughed. She liked being Shampy. It sounded larky.

Real friends groaned at the same things and got the giggles together. They approved each other's Honour Marks, and sympathised when homework had to be repeated, like the girl's attempt at drawing a section from a map with contours that seemed less real than *Crossroads*. Dougi, who sang and played guitar, could tell whether music went up or down and how much; the girl couldn't. But friends made it fun to be clueless. Being top in English, and sometimes in History or Religious Knowledge, was a different feeling and the best kind for sharing at home but it was embarrassing at the same time. Most things that happened outside lessons were private, like the jokes that only existed between the three of them, and the words grown-ups didn't use, like *outasite* and *for yonks*.

The girl had friends in the Sixth Form. That was because of lunchtime clubs, where the tall, kind girls who mostly wanted to be teachers or nurses thought she was cheeky but nice, and she felt like a favourite. One of the Sixth Formers who ran Junior Christian Union called her Jimi, after Hendrix, because of her big hair and full lips. The girl didn't know much about Hendrix except chart positions for a few songs that were too wild for her, but she thought it was a much hipper nickname than Shampy when you wrote it down. So when she entered the school creative writing competition, she used it as her pen name. Her story was a kind of mystery but not violent. She hoped it would win like her story when she was seven, the one about horses. The prizes were awarded in assembly one day by Mr S who mostly taught exam classes and directed Shakespeare plays. When he stood up at the front of the hall to read out the winners in front of the whole school, she felt as if her breath was held up against the buffers.

"In third place," he said, "is Jirni." He waited. She was too upset to work it out at first. Then when no one else made her way onto the stage, she realised. Only it felt almost as bad as wonderful, as if her writing, which had won a Basildon Bond competition when she was ten, was no good any more. Or the story wasn't really hers. Or the hall would be full of puzzled faces that meant *huh?*

But people applauded as Mr S said she was one of the youngest entrants and shook her hand. "Very well done." She felt high as Lucy in the sky with diamonds. But it was hard to feel shiny, and lumpy and frizzy, at the same time. She didn't find the voice to say, "It's Jimi, after Hendrix," in case the pretty girls, the made-up girls and the skinhead girls sniggered. Because she wasn't hip at all. And when he asked for her real name, it sounded like it came from *Janet and John*.

But her friends were nearly as happy as Dad. For her twelfth birthday party, her top ten friends came to the house and thought he was nearly as funny as Eric Morecambe because he made up games no one else in the world had ever played before, and dangled sweets on strings from the bedroom window. So it didn't matter about not having a car. And someone said he was handsome too, like Gregory Peck. So she said, "He's a poet," and they were amazed.

It was a shame Mum and Dad only liked the girls who smiled and spoke nicely. Some girls were just shy with grown-ups, like she was. And some people's parents smoked and drank, danced to pop music and went to football matches, said *ruddy thing* and dropped aitches. It didn't mean they were bad influences even though she could tell Mum thought so.

Friends were like a secret really, and you kept them for life.

—— *Cy* ——

When *Sam and Cy* reformed after a two-year break, we began to work the comedy circuit. There were some crazy comedians and clubs out there. I remember *Pear-shaped* in Fitzrovia, run by Brian Damage, had a teddy bear on a pulley that moved along above your head either quickly if you were *dying* or slowly if you got laughs. There was a fabulously bohemian and manic edge to the place which suited us well. We shifted between our wedding speech as Trevor and Sheila from Essex to our criminal brothers Frank and Bern, and we rarely died. Another club, *Ivan's Comedy Gaff* was probably both the worst and best in town. Ivan the Comedy

Ref (dressed as a football referee) was the host and seemed to take great pleasure in killing any laughs, which was at times hilarious as he confused and berated the audience. On his Edinburgh flyer it said *Madman or genius?* I remember one poor chap attempting to heckle; I think he wanted his £5 back. Ivan sat down beside him and asked him where he was from.

"Bognor."

Paraphrasing the last words of King George V, Ivan retorted, "F**k Bognor!"

The man left with Ivan shouting this after him down the road.

My friend Dan was there that night to see Sam and me and he always loved to recall this anarchic attack upon the audience. Comedy is an extremely strange science. We were constantly re-writing material in between shows if it didn't work. But occasionally if we had a longer set we'd go right back to our surreal karate/mask-pulling off and in some places this went down a storm. We had our best gig, our worst gig and our most mediocre gig all in the same venue with the same set. Which seemed to prove that you just needed to stick to your guns and believe in your material and your audience would find you.

Still, our agent, Nigel, was quite tough and insisted that some of the more surreal material and some of our characters had to go. "You need more gags – gag-gag-gag," was a phrase I will always remember and one that Sam often repeated in an extremely funny impression. We had been looking for a guiding principle and a structure for the show and in true *Sam and Cy* fashion with the character of our agent we'd found it. We decided that he would be the voice of *God* on stage and a bright spotlight would stop us mid-sketch and the agent's voice would interrupt us. "What is this rubbish? You need more gags." The sheer cheek and bravery of it made us and our audiences laugh and I don't remember Nigel ever mentioning it. It was around this time in fact that he felt the show was ready to take to Edinburgh.

Sue

"You're kind, darling, and you've got a very good brain," said Mum. "You told me you had more Honour Marks last term than anyone!"

A lot of people didn't bother any more to queue at lunchtime to get theirs signed by the Headmistress who lived in her office and dressed like the Queen Mother. Some girls smoked behind the bike shed and wore mascara and heels. Two girls in the Lower Fifth had left to have babies, and they were both pretty enough to date a Rolling Stone.

"I'd rather be beautiful than clever!"

George Eliot would have understood, but her mother didn't. She didn't think she meant it. But what was the point of writing essays that earned her A, when poets were drawn to beauty, not girls who were size 16 with frizzy hair and freckles? When everything worth reading was about love, and no one would ever want to marry her?

"You wouldn't really," said her mother.

The girl knew she was disappointed. She remembered the time she came back from supporting the netball team at a tournament with brown eye shadow, thanks to one of the skinhead girls who told her in the Ladies that her eyes were really blue. She'd had to wash it off because make-up made her shallow and cheap. And on the school trip to France she'd been the only one whose parents wouldn't sign their permission for her to have a glass of wine at dinner. Mum didn't even approve of the blue glass cross she bought on the last day at Sacré Coeur, because faith was a quiet, serious thing, not for show.

Other mothers wore miniskirts and lipstick, drove cars and drank Campari. Hers changed the channel if characters swore or were unfaithful. She used to say she'd fight off a tiger to save her children, and they believed her. When she was twenty-one and the other teachers at her first school *ran the Headmaster down* in the staff room, she told them all, "If you have grievances why don't you tell him to his face, instead of behind his back?"

The girl wanted that kind of courage. She hoped one day she'd stop caring about anything but God, peace and justice. She wrote poems about Apartheid, drug addiction, suicide, starving children and war, and made herself cry. She imagined herself suffering a hunger strike until the world abandoned nuclear weapons. Her father's shyness hadn't prevented him declaring himself a Conscientious Objector, and making a speech to justify his conviction. That was the finest, hardest courage for a man who doubted everything, especially himself, and avoided cameras, parties and centre stage. A man who, at boarding school, had been unable to save his brother who died of Meningitis.

It was easier to be brave in stories but death was even more moving. She was writing a novel about a plain, Christian girl who married a poet with Cat Stevens hair and bare feet. She loved him and his talent completely, but he killed himself when the world didn't want his poems or his peace.

"In any case," said her mother, "you have a lovely face."

"I don't," said the girl, trying not to let her voice break over something so selfish and trivial and stupid, but she knew love was meant to be blind. She counted on it.

—— *Cy* ——

Edinburgh during the festival always felt like a homecoming to me. A place where I belonged. From the streets filled with performers and music and people dressed in costumes to the bars and clubs, the atmosphere is vibrant and there's a palpable excitement.
I have a memory of staying up all night drinking and finally getting to the Penny Black, a bar that opened at five in the morning. As I walked back to where we were staying, after a couple for the road, the sound of bagpipes and the outline of the castle rose out of the early morning mist. I remember thinking this was it. I was here. I had made it. Not fame and fortune. But just this moment. I bathed in it. Again it was a moment before and after, at the beginning and the end.
I had many such moments in Edinburgh.
Sam had almost not made it with a throat infection that plagued him on and off for years and always seemed to flare up when he was under stress. It hit him really badly just before Edinburgh and I had promised not to smoke in the flat we shared. Which was how I met the enchanting Stairwell Girl. She had long black hair and a lovely smile and we spent lots of time talking, smoking and sneaking out on the town against my agent's orders. The time we talked on the stairwell was another *time outside time* for me.

BEHIND THE MASK

—— *Leslie* ——

My ugly sister tells me she isn't my friend. She's the eye in the mirror who sees what's wrong. My ugly sister says I'm old and I'm a panto man squeezed into a dress. My ugly sister notices the too-large hands, the Adam's apple, the policeman's feet.

When I'm with my ugly sister, nothing fits. The shoes are too tight, the dresses won't zip up, the waistbands slip down. Standing next to her I'm oversize and blokey. She's the person who sees me stride into action talking loudly about how to park a car.

My ugly sister shaves off stubble till the cuts appear. She's the reason I don't go sleeveless or wear short skirts. My ugly sister crosses the road to avoid old men and school kids. She tells me to be careful of drivers who might mount the pavement and run me down.

My ugly sister is and isn't who I am.

My beautiful boy wears a pink dress with a blue lace collar and a bow at the back. Inside the dress he lives in a room full of stars and painted birds. He's me smelling flowers and asking for their names. Now I'm walking with my mum to the shops where the voices are loud and the faces lit up. Everything's busy and surprising. When we're out in the park, people take notice and I smile like a girl. I'm in a dream, my mum says as we make our way home.

My beautiful boy plays upstairs in an imaginary dress. No one else can see it. When he comes downstairs he's got it on, when he helps with the housework he's still wearing it, when he makes up stories the dress is there too. He wears it at school when he gets ten out of ten, and on his walk home. The dress is with him when he eats supper and when he says his prayers, and in his dreams.

My beautiful boy has a book he's reading, hidden in his bed. It's called *The Emperor's Dress*. It's a tale of transformation. In his version, the king's a magician and the boy's his assistant. When the drums roll he's sawn in half, popping back up afterwards in a swimsuit. He makes up other stories, light bulb moments with talk in the head and girl-boy switches. There are voices, obsessions and golden memories. My beautiful boy's on the cover of *The Emperor's Dress*. He's writing these words.

—— *Sue* ——

There were two girls in the class who became friends because neither of them fitted in. Lynne was buxom, with Cleopatra eyes and a haircut from the future. She just about tolerated school with her head tilted and her mouth hanging open in a sulk that was nearly a yawn. Lynne made uniform glamorous but Jane made it as dowdy as possible. Lynne could have passed for twenty-eight when she was sixteen; Jane reminded the girl of Virginia Woolf as a scullery maid. Neither of them bothered to speak much to anyone else, including the teachers in class. The girl was wary of Lynne, who didn't seem to see or hear her, or care what she was missing. She worried for Jane, who seemed so timid, pale and nervy that she might have been thinking of loading her pockets with stones and wading into a river.

In English everyone was meant to prepare a short scene for two and act it. The girl was eager to write a script but appalled by the idea of standing in front of the class, where everyone would see how fat, frizzy and embarrassing she was, even before she tried to speak. There had been a time when she'd played Sir Francis Drake in her own production, but that past wasn't just another country; it seemed to belong to another girl. Now when she was asked to read the part of Macbeth it felt like a blow to the chest. She'd rather run from the room and throw up in the Girls' Toilets.

The teacher looked at the register, and called on Lynne and Jane – who disappeared to change, and shuffled back in torn, old-man clothes, with dirty, old-man faces. They mumbled and grunted. Their lines were like Pinter. No one knew whether to laugh or gawp but everyone was mesmerised, even before the two characters cut open a can of cold baked beans and ate them by the spoonful. With their mouths open as they talked, they showed orange teeth gummed and dripping. Sauce dribbled down their chins and streaked their shirts and jackets. Lynne wiped her mouth with her cuff. Jane tipped the can and her head, and let the contents fall into her lap and slide into her hair. All the while they kept talking, as if their world was theirs alone and their words had a private meaning, or none.

The girl had never seen anything so daring, so outrageous or so dark. She had never imagined what it must be like to do something so far beyond people's expectations, and not to care what they thought.

Her own sketch would be nothing now because she knew nothing. She still lived in a nest.

A few months later Lynne was off school for half a term, and the rumour was that the hospital was *a mental home*. The girl and her friends included Jane at breaks and lunchtimes, and sometimes at weekends too. They liked her. But even though Jane praised her poems, the girl was uneasy. Her imagination wasn't elastic enough to imagine what Jane might do. She was used to other girls and their parents drawing lines in different places. But Jane had different lines and sometimes none at all.

She was a risk, and that was something the girl couldn't take. Not in life, only in stories.

—— *Leslie* ——

I used to believe in the woman within. I felt, when I cross-dressed, closer to my feminine side – though what I experienced was more a release of pressure, a kind of pleasurable lift as if I was walking out after being indoors for a month. *Relief dressing* was good for me; it increased my sensitivity, making me softer, calmer and more alive. And to dress in front of others required a special kind of tuning out, a deliberately willed blindness where I didn't ask questions. I was on display but chose not to know it. Though, of course, I was vulnerable. It was as if I'd been turned inside out, with all my feelings on show. And it was that exposure that both set me apart and made me strong.

My position was simple. I believed I was being more honest than the other men, the straight guys, who had the same feelings but were afraid to show them. In my private imaginings they were the stern men of action who kept at a distance and always wore a mask. But my attempts to pull rank didn't get far. The men I had in mind simply shrugged their shoulders and carried on with their business, remarking casually that it didn't bother them. Perhaps I *wanted* a reaction, a kind of reverse validation where they showed their dislike, or told me I was being stupid.

Sometimes we thrive on rejection. I found that being in opposition gave me definition and made me seem strong – even to myself. There was a magic about it, an inner frisson from being alive and untouchable; and while I was taking my stand, I knew who I was.

But there were other voices inside, telling me to stay hidden.

It would be easier. I was fearful of what men might do; that once I was known I might be followed and given *the treatment*. In my mind I saw broken glass, paint sprays and blood on the doorstep.

Part of me believed that my appearance jarred. To some people it might seem deliberately provocative, as if I was shouting, "Look at me!" For a few of them – potential bullies, abusers, rapists – I was asking for it.

My sensible self told me that women's clothes were impractical and designed for a different body shape. They were to keep girls girlie and obsessed with appearance.

There was an analysis that explained it all in terms of stepping down from a position of male power. It was a contrary act, similar to the French aristos dressing up as shepherds at Versailles.

I was a child in a gown. Sooner or later I'd grow up.

But of course it wouldn't go away or stay hidden.

I had plenty of time to get used to my trans-self, from the private struggles of youth, through my *harmless* dressing in the house, to being outed by the papers and appearing in public. I learned on the way that going public is a continuous effort – and who wants to live on permanent emergency callout? Because to keep up an effective presence involves a high-energy readiness to deal with other people's reactions, fielding anything from awkward looks to rude jokes and direct challenges. It's oh-so much easier to blend in, put on a suit and walk around being *normal*.

And it's natural to go through phases, sometimes standing up to be counted and sometimes ducking out.

But as long as part of me remained undercover I could only see myself as a *rara avis*, defined by being other. And my negation went deep. So for much of the time I was a functioning doer and achiever, but when it came to self, I lacked connection or inner balance. Like a child in an exam, I was too busy – or nervous – to understand what was happening.

To give a few examples:
1. Much like the so-called straight guys I worked flat out. Nothing could stop me, my purpose was to get things done. And to go home at night having dealt with several major crises gave me a purpose.
2. I was expressive, but not in *that way*. I'd learned at school that being effeminate was a no-no. Being caught out smelling flowers or reading poetry soon led to attacks, so it was better to keep my girliness hidden.
3. As a young adult, I used diversionary tactics. So I'd shout rather than cry, speak out, laugh and be energetic, keeping up a pumped-up front – especially to myself.

Even when I went public, I still felt brittle and exposed. I imagined people were watching and passing judgement. In a sense I didn't quite know where to put myself.

I do remember a couple of incidents.

In one, we were celebrating an election win at our house and the rooms were full of left-wing Labour friends. I have a memory of dancing downstairs to thunderous music, wearing high heels and a long kaftan. As a tall man, I was aware – and secretly proud of – the balancing act required. Part of me was dancing in darkness just for its own sake, and part of me wanted to be admired and show what I could do. I felt safe in this company to strut my stuff.

Later, during a visit to the toilet, I realised my mistake. On the way there I passed J, a councillor I'd campaigned with. He was young and slightly-built with red hair and a foxy, rather guarded expression. When I returned to the landing he was standing in a doorway next to his girlfriend, watching me. I could see he had something to say so I got in first, telling a story involving a mutual friend. J looked me up and down as if he hadn't heard a word.

"What's this about?" he said. His eyes had hardened, but he was grinning.

I knew what he meant but chose to put it off. "You enjoying the party?" I asked, mildly.

"Why you like that?" he asked.

"How do you mean?" In him I could see the tough kids staring at me with their fists clenched.

"Why you wearing that?"

"Why?"

"Yes, why?"

"It's my choice."

"But what for?"

"What for? For nothing. For myself."

"It doesn't suit."

"Bloody hell."

"You shouldn't be like that. Looks wrong."

Shrugging, I began to walk away, but then turned back. I couldn't leave it. He'd got under my skin, and the anger made me hot and breathless. "Piss off," I hissed. "You wouldn't dare say that to a woman."

Behind that statement was so much he couldn't understand. My childhood fears, the inner flirtation with being a woman; most of all, my balance between confusion and defiance.

I think I surprised him. At school, saying that guaranteed a beating, but he didn't call out or come after me, so perhaps he wasn't absolutely serious. Looking back now, I think I should have talked to him.

In the other incident I was standing in a pub with a group of friends. I was wearing jeans and a red, flower-patterned blouse. I remember two men by the bar, staring hard and exchanging remarks. There was a ha-ha sneeriness about them, a kind of chin-out invitation directed at me. I knew their purpose was to weaken me. The pub was their territory, and their hard, threatening stares said *keep out*.

Nobody else noticed, and I didn't tell my friends. I was ashamed, and thought, or hoped, I might be mistaken. But my own shakiness was a reminder of bullying at school. When we left, I wanted people by me, but I didn't have the courage to admit it. We drifted back to the cars in ones and twos, with everyone enjoying themselves except me. The men didn't follow and nothing happened, but I felt their stares for a long time afterwards. In a way, they'd won.

Then there were the stories of other people.

My friend R was driven out of her estate when a group of youths discovered she was trans. They lay in wait every evening when she came home from work. Fortunately, she was able to move out before their threats turned to violence.

When I visited a trans pub in Islington I was warned about police arrests and body searches.

At the same pub there were people who had lost friends, loved ones and jobs.

Many trans people I've met have, like me, come through self-esteem issues and addiction problems after repeated attempts to *kick the habit*.

But of course people survive, and all of them were supported by close friends or by family.

Nowadays I'm more out in public. It's the result of writing a book and having to live up to it. Of course, fitting the real self to an image isn't always easy, and words narrow life, but it gives me a framed space where people can look in and ask questions – and they do, in their heads. It's a place I go back to where I'm in the picture as both subject and object. The world's out there, people are walking back and forth, sometimes they're staring or waving, but I'm quite comfortable. They're guests at my party, seeing me as I am, and if they don't like it, the loss is theirs.

And the men?

I understand now their jokes and resistance, their willingness to *do*. For most men, what I wear doesn't matter, they're direct and fair-minded and life's more important. And I've been cross-dressed in shopping malls and on trains with football supporters and had lots of support from caring men who act independently without fear or favour. Admittedly, there are still a few blokey blokes whose looks scare me. But I tell myself to keep walking and look the other way because I can feel my hot male anger bubbling up – and that's not how I want to be. But of course, if I'm honest, there's always a macho somewhere inside. I can swear and shout like the next man, the only difference is that for me it's more important to recognise the man *and* the woman inside, to talk about them and know them, to be non-binary and not be afraid.

—— *Sue* ——

Dad's work shirt hung on the handle of her door, like an intruder. Mum insisted on putting clothes there to air after ironing, and the girl could hardly say, at her age, that it gave her the creeps. Just as she couldn't explain how deeply, how fervently, she wished she hadn't seen that film at the cinema: *Out of Time*, with Jack the Ripper. Period dramas weren't all Jane Austen after all. And she'd thought it would be detective work as well as time travel. She'd imagined, now that she was reading adult novels that secretly shocked her, and enjoying Mum's disapproval of some of them, that she could handle it. Kidding herself again. Because the terror of the victims was worse, in anticipation of the knife, than the gore itself, and all of it had become part of her in a way she couldn't change. It would cling, like that stupid panto Ogre, long after she'd forgotten theorems and capital cities. And now she was scared of Dad's shirt!

Turning in the darkness towards the window and the garage it overlooked, she began picturing a man, not with a cloak but jeans, climbing onto its roof as a stepping stone to her bedroom. There were men who did that, to women. And it would be like a dream where she screamed harder than ever before but all that burst out was silence. She told herself everyone dreamed that, not just teenage girls the teachers called *sensitive*. They didn't all dream of the stairs, like a ship's ladder, that Dad designed to take the bungalow up to attic bedrooms, falling into space as she climbed them. How many times? And he'd be so hurt, as if she had no faith in him, when she trusted him more than anyone.

But the local police never found the murderer who stabbed an old couple on Jane's road – green and peaceful, with trees blossoming and neat front lawns. Rippers pretended to be husbands, brothers and fathers. How could she sleep without a killer filling her bedroom window, knife in hand and blinding her with torchlight? And how could she tell Dad he shouldn't have built the garage there, when they didn't even have a car? She was too sensible for this. Wasn't she loved? Wasn't she clever? Didn't other people forget the news for supper and *Coronation Street*?

She rolled over and pressed her face hard into the pillow until she saw lights like firework fountains. Characters in *Sons and Lovers* didn't lie awake at night imagining murderers dead or alive. They were too busy with real feelings. She was sorriest for Walter Morel, because he needed to be loved, really loved, and Gertrude's love was stifling. It kept him small. She remembered the A for her last essay and the way she made Dougi and Pea laugh with a joke she couldn't even remember. Some kind of clowning anyway.

Did imagination make her immature? She could ask Dad about that but he hated it when she put herself down, like he did, as if it was catching. Sunday had been one of his bad days. That was the worst kind of darkness, when she dreamed of Daddy dying. Finding him, and knowing he was too sad to live.

―― *Leslie* ――

And now, when I walk into town I'm wearing a dress. It's long and flowery with bunched sleeves and an underslip. There are two of me walking. The person in the dress is saying hello to the man at the flower stall and the woman in trainers; the person inside is two-spirit and apart.

I'm keeping it as simple as I can. I'm very so-whatish; crazy as well – standout, wildcard, absurd – but I choose not to know it. I hear Bowie singing *Rebel, Rebel*. I think of pink roses, butterflies and Expressionist paintings. At this age I can smile.

When it comes to how people see me, I know the difference. With women it's a glance and a smile; with men it's eyes down and a quickening of step.

I've developed an interest in pattern, colour and matching accessories.

I browse women's clothes in shop windows.

I know how outfits can be too hot or too cold, depending on weather.

I understand now why it takes women so long to get out of the house. It's the switching of keys from one bag to another, the layers to wear, poppers to pop, shoes to buckle and a scarf or hanky or gloves left behind.

I'm in my element in a dress.

In women's clothes I'm on stage. It's a marked-out space, a charmed circle.

Inside me, there's a blurring of gender lines.

It's an act of imagination.

Sue

It was a hot July day but her legs weren't slim enough for a mini skirt. Instead she wore brown bell bottom loons, cheap from Milletts and paid for with her Saturday wages from the bookshop. Her top was vivid orange and probably didn't suit skin inclined to flush. In a year's time she'd be in the hall with an examination number, but this lunchtime she was in a stock room with no window and five chairs rammed in close together. *Writers' Circle* was select. And he called her a writer. She sat closest to him, because she'd arrived first, along with Jane who knew. Who'd guessed before she told anyone.

"You're in love with Mr S, aren't you?"

As if it was normal as well as obvious. Not a Thomas Hardy novel where someone or something had to die. But not a silly thing either, not a crush.

The cupboard smelt of paper, dust and summer. Piled on a shelf she noticed *Sons and Lovers*, and remembered how he'd talked about the lilies, the swing – about passion, and tenderness too. It felt almost secret, being there with him – and with the poem, typed and folded, waiting on her lap. The girl tried to care what Jane had written because it would be strange and perhaps disturbing, as hard to understand as a great poem could be. For the two Upper Fifths with their smooth, matching bunches, it was only their second time. She hoped they wouldn't try to rhyme again. That was so awkward. She didn't know why people did it, unless they were Wordsworth or Auden.

He talked, joked, searched for books, checked his watch. He was always rushed but that was because of his energy for everything that made school wonderful. Not just his lessons but the plays and the panel games at lunchtimes that packed the hall because of him: his animation and humour, the expectation of surprises. She loved the way his face re-shaped and his voice had warmth and tempo, his hands dancing. Not fine hands like Dad's, but boyish, playful. His hair was boyish too, wiry and thick with curls. She imagined the curls around her fingers. She knew his smell, not smoky or sweaty but earth and water and mints. She watched his mouth, never still, quick to smile and laugh and celebrate, but also to respond, like his body, to the words. Hers.

In her poem he was just a pronoun. But everything: the whole, the inspiration, the theme and form. He was her vocabulary. She woke with her head full of it, until at bedtime she lay wondering whether he might think of her too, just for a moment, and smile. Whether he told his wife, "There's a girl who could be talented, I think. Painfully shy but full of soul." She didn't picture his body. The only men she'd seen naked were Greek gods in galleries and he would be imperfectly human. He wouldn't see her as flesh. But she hoped he found her, the true and silent self, in her essays and her eyes. When he talked about Shakespeare or Ted Hughes, his spirit surged and sang through every line.

In her imagination she had kissed him, again and again. And then like Jane Eyre she had fled, crying. He was too good a man for that.

The Upper Fifth pair apologised and sat.

"No, no, glad you came! You're all a miracle."

He looked at her. It was an invitation. But if she read her poem first, she would have to sit immobilised by the weight of it until the bell rang. Her body heat would rise and keep rising as she heard it again, replayed the words, their sound, his face, his hands. His thoughts, echoing.

"All right," she said.

Jane might be looking at her, excited perhaps. Head down, she must begin. As if he wasn't there. The words that had survived were as simple as she could manage. "Be authentic," he'd said, "and direct. No fancy ornaments."

Afraid she was mumbling at speed, she paused. Looking up she glimpsed his face before she turned back to the paper. His living face, intent, respectful, kind.

"He cut through my life," she read.

"Never dreaming of the shreds he left behind."

She folded it away and looked towards the open door onto the corridor. A couple of girls passed by, laughing. Back in the stock room, one of the Upper Fifths clapped and the other joined in. Jane smiled encouragingly. All four faces turned to his.

"I applaud your courage," he said, serious and gentle. "You've moved us and that's always a gift. Thank you."

She coloured. He must guess. How could he not?

"I'd like to hear it again, if you're willing ...?"

Her mouth twitched into lines she couldn't hold.

"Maybe at the end," he suggested. "Thank you, Susan." And he clapped too, just a couple of times, quick and quiet.

She hoped he knew.

"*I love you, love you, love you,*" she told him with her eyes, until they brimmed.

"*Susan, Sue, dear Sue. If I were free ... I'm so sorry. I won't forget you.*" Words he would never say, hands that would never touch.

She would like to die. But she was alive.

—— Cy ——

When I was a schoolboy I used to get myself sent to the Headmistress so I could watch the fish in her aquarium. The buzzing of the tank and the fluorescent glow of the window to an underwater world filled me with awe.

And I'd imagine that if I could pass through that transparent wall I would find myself floating in an undersea city. Atlantis – a lost paradise of barnacle-encrusted pillars and spires where the bells were rung by the ocean's current.

There was a Clownfish in there flitting about and some remarkable half-yellow half-blue fish like tiny flat cats' eyes, darting in a swirling shoal, making patterns like the letters of some forgotten alphabet.

Finally the desire to enter this world overwhelmed me and I removed my uniform, lifted off the heavy black plastic lid and climbed in. To my surprise, my feet were not met by the coloured stones that covered the bottom, but floated freely. And as I lowered myself down my entire body was completely submerged. I took a gulp of air and let go of the sides. There I was, inside. Looking out I could see the reception area, the bookshelves, the trophy cabinet, the class photos.

It was warm in there, like swimming in soft syrup, and as I watched, the door of the headmistress' office, so far away as if in dream time, opened to reveal a rectangle of light from which the headmistress strode. She looked like a doll. A tiny toy headmistress in a tiny room. There was no fearing her now, now that I'd escaped. The whole idea of school was like some strange game dreamt up in a story book. A vision of an alien world viewed through a microscope.

I realised then that I too was a Clownfish. I have remained in that fish tank, never wishing to escape its transparent walls.

IN THE ASYLUM

—— *Cy* ——

The arched ceiling in Sam Ball's Occupational Therapy Department at the hospital was made up of a network of hexagons like the interior of a hive. At the end of the corridor behind a thick, battered, bottle-green door was what used to be a padded cell. One could still see where the pads had been removed. Despite the fact that the majority of his clients were either severely demented or otherwise disorientated, Sam's attempts to use the space for managing the group had failed. All refused to cross the threshold.

One day, when my group had finished early, I walked over to see Sam and met a woman being taken back to her ward. She was staring at me with a wide rictus grin stretched around nicotine-stained teeth. "I'm going home for Christmas," she said. I later found out that her husband had admitted her to the hospital sometime in the 70s and never returned.

Sam asked for another pair of hands to move some chairs into a storage room at the end of the corridor. Of course I was happy to help. As I stepped into what had been the padded cell I felt a cold shiver travel up my spine. There was a strange, ghostly electricity in the air. "Did you feel anything?" he asked me afterwards. I said I had. It was then he told me about what it had been and the refusal of his patients to enter.

There was a tree rooted in cracked concrete on the forecourt of the ward where my department was situated. Its shape reminded me of twisted limbs and faces silently crying out. It was no surprise to me that shortly after I began work there I arrived one morning to find it had been cut down. The hospital authorities had realised that this 3D Arthur Rackham illustration was not a good advertisement for modern mental health care.

The psychiatric hospital was a place of painfully beautiful tragedy. You felt the pain in the huge pea-green corridors and in the eyes of its inhabitants. I drew a picture of one of my patients at the time like a little girl, lost and alone in a jungle. Madness, it seemed to me, was like a big cat. Its approach was terrifying, but once in its warm belly, there was a peacefulness about it, an acceptance. The outside world couldn't hurt you anymore.

The patient I had drawn was Miss Cole. On our first meeting, Miss Cole made a beeline for me. Fears have a way of doing that, I find. If you're scared of dogs they approach you, if it's wasps they seek you out, and no sooner had I set foot on the ward than a tiny figure in a loose-fitting hospital gown and huge felted granny slippers scooted across the polished floor toward me. She was twirling a wooden spoon in her hand and speaking fast.

Miss Cole pushed herself right up against me. Her voice was the clipped plummy English-type voice I'd heard so often in black-and-white films. She was like a radio. A time radio. That's the only way I can describe it. The thoughts flowed out and the information flowed in with no regard for past, present or future. So she talked about a butcher's shop long ago and her sister in the front room watching television as she introduced herself to me wondering who I was, as I seemed like an interesting young man, although I should get my hair cut and stand up straight and did I know what was for lunch ... and the butcher said he had beef but she'd already brought the mint sauce and the programme was awful, the acting so wooden, so they decided to turn it off in the end and listen to some music on the radio and have some Jacob's cream crackers and a cup of tea ...

I stared at her, fascinated. Her mind was wide open. My first instinct was to take her in my arms and look after her. She was vulnerable in a way that others would not understand ... and they would destroy her beauty, medicalise her miracle. It was a light bulb moment, similar to falling in love and had Miss Cole been 40 years younger, perhaps we would have run away together. But what we both saw, as I began to learn how to interact with her, was that we were soul mates. A double act. Yes, another double act.

I don't think what I achieved in the ward in those first few months would have been possible without Miss Cole.

Each day she'd be there, helping me round up the clients for my Occupational Therapy Group, twirling the walking stick that had replaced the wooden spoon of our first encounter. As I stood at the blackboard chalking up the patients' ideas, she would be by my side, chipping in with her random, wide-ranging general knowledge. We laughed a lot. Our daily programmes sidestepped the officially prescribed programme of old-time music and Beetle Drives – although Miss Cole and I occasionally put our own twist on these activities if we were due a visit from the powers that be. Instead we played games, some of which I would use later with my son, such as indoor *Silly Cricket* in which we made up the rules as we went along. We created wall murals of beach scenes with giant ice creams and flying parasols and teapots. The patients taught me how to cook and we all scoffed more than our fair share of biscuits in tea-breaks, with discussions about the state of the world that sometimes lasted an entire afternoon.

When the time came for Miss Cole to leave the hospital, I remember arriving on the ward to find she was nowhere to be seen. A nurse told me she had been on a home visit and had *retired to her bed*. The curtains were closed around it and I coughed politely outside.

"Is that you Mr Henty?"

"Yes Miss Cole."

"That's OK then, you may come in."

Miss Cole was laid upon her bed with her eyes half-closed and her cheeks smeared with a sticky brown substance.

She offered me a chocolate digestive. "I smuggled them back from my home visit. You won't tell them?"

Them, I thought ... it was always *them* for Miss Cole. The authorities. She was anarchic, simply because she had to be.

On her last day we sat in the courtyard looking up at the planes crisscrossing the sky and came up with a plan to stop time altogether. We talked and talked and it was only when I heard a tapping on the window that I realised my working day was done.

It was Sam. "Is that your friend?"

"Yes."

I turned to Miss Cole, "I'd better go, I guess. Goodbye Miss Cole."

I did see her again, twice. When a colleague of mine had to take her shopping, Miss Cole had requested I go along, and begrudgingly *they* had agreed. At our meeting, Miss Cole clasped my hand and began to ice-skate in her slippers across the polished floor of the shopping centre. It must have looked very strange to the other shoppers: this tall, gangly long-haired 21 year-old and miniature old lady gliding across the floor to unheard classical music.

The second time, she was refusing to take the depot injection of her anti-psychotic. *They* decided to drive me out to her house to see if I could persuade her. Her house was a terrace which reminded me of Mr Benn's from the 70's children's television series and in my mind she will always live in *Festive Road*. Inside, there was an old wireless and the pictures and decor looked like they hadn't changed since the 1940s. Miss Cole sat at the dining table on a wooden chair and a burly, red-faced nurse was in the middle of arguing with her about taking her medication. I'd never heard Miss Cole use bad language but in this case she was fiercely abusive – in the midst of which she fixed me with one mischievously glinting black pupil. "Have you eaten yet?" she said. This will be my abiding memory of this beautiful, wild woman.

I met other characters in the hospital at that time.

The Ballerina gliding, phantom-like, through the ward in a diaphanous shift of pure white. She waltzed with an invisible partner to the music in her mind, pirouetting with delicate grace. Her eyes were like polished obsidian. She was beautiful and bright and sharp as a blade of glass.

Cyril, the slight man with braces, who'd been a ship's cook. I can see his crumpled face beneath his neatly Brylcreemed white hair – always preoccupied, though doing his best to engage. "S'cuse me," he'd say in his dulcet cockney tones, "I've got a stew on the go," and he'd nip out to the ward and his imaginary galley. Finding it didn't exist, he'd excuse himself and search the Occupational Therapy Department. Not finding his galley there either, he'd sit for a time before repeating the process, over and over.

I remember feeling very hurt when I finally came across a patient I couldn't seem to form a bond with. She was a lady who believed that some men were werewolves. I've always been reasonably hairy and that, unfortunately, triggered her terrible obsession, causing her to refuse to join my group.

The consultant psychiatrist was Dr Bodhi, which is the name of the sacred tree under which the Buddha sat, sometimes translated as *Awakening* or *Enlightenment*. He was a very genteel and intelligent man and, although I was unqualified, always listened intently to my views on the patients during Ward Round.

Once Dr Bodhi had to deal with a new admission, a well-known politician and businessman who'd forced through a lot of questionable deals and legislation before turning up in the middle of the night at a colleague's house completely naked, demanding that he be taken seriously. The bizarre thing about him was that he was utterly convincing. As soon as he arrived on the ward he began talking, coherently and believably, about how his colleagues had him admitted to *get him out of the way* and that when he got out he was going to sue them and *make them pay.*

In Ward Round I told Dr Bodhi that he seemed coherent and orientated, bright and alert.

"Bring him in," the doctor said and talked to him for much longer than usual, taking on board what he said, agreeing that it was a serious matter and would be looked into. The session went on and on and I couldn't for the life of me understand why he would keep the man talking for so long. However, eventually the man suddenly rolled up the leg of his trousers to reveal, in large letters scrawled in biro on his shin, the words *I am not insane.*

'There, there you see! Isn't that proof enough?" he cried.
"Yes," said Dr Bohdi, "I think you've answered my question."

People in a manic state are often charming, charismatic and able to access parts of the brain that are usually closed off, meaning that they can display a supreme level of intelligence and recall in order to outwit other people. I've seen an elderly lady in this state throw four nurses around like corks in water; but the low that follows can be fathoms deep. I remember this politician not long afterwards struggling to gather the energy to tie his own shoelaces, hardly able to interact at all. The boundaries of behaviour are drawn differently with people who go against the norm, and certainly not always easy to see. Was Miss Cole more of a danger to the world than a corrupt politician in charge of vast parts of it? In Douglas Adam's *Hitchhikers Guide* series he has a man called *Wonko the Sane* who lives in an inside-out house on a beach and has put the whole world in an asylum.

A man arrived on the ward in a pressed suit, shirt, tie, tie-pin and shiny black loafers. His hair was neatly combed, his manner reserved and courteous. He presented as an extremely *straight* and *upright* member of the community. It turned out that his recent retirement had given him more time to dress up in his wife's clothes, a pleasure he'd always enjoyed in secret. Unfortunately his wife had discovered him cross-dressed and, horrified, had called their son who, also horrified, had alerted their daughter. They'd had a family meeting where everyone agreed that he was in the middle of a mental breakdown, perhaps as a result of his retirement. He'd gone along with their idea rather than admitting that this was a lifetime habit, and had promised that he would seek treatment. I had to wonder what kind of world it was that required this poor man to claim insanity in order to placate the ignorance of his own family.

I felt my heart ache daily for my patients as if there was a huge sponge in there soaking up the pain. I was a naïve young man who worked simply to support becoming a professional comedian, but the inability to distance myself that made me, I believe, supremely good at my job, also made it an impossibility. The hospital was vast. The corridors seemed designed for giants, stretching for miles with empty rooms and departments, deserted staircases and lifts, like an unknown city after an apocalyptic event. I remember getting lost on the way to pick up a patient from *Art Therapy*, a place I'd never heard of. The patient was *Arfur*. He was extremely tall and thin, like an elongated ectomorphic shadow at sunset. Covered in tattoos, with a pallid, stubbly face and NHS spectacles perched on an aquiline nose, Arfur was a contortionist. He could twist his limbs and his fingers into impossible knots as if he were a piece of string. In this condition the adrenaline pulsed through his body, making his lips quiver and his fingers vibrate, so that he constantly bit them to keep them still. Arfur was a compulsive clock-watcher who chain smoked. His job was to lay the cutlery for mealtimes each day. Who gave him this task, or whether he gave it to himself as some kind of penance I don't know, but it made it impossible for him to focus on anything else. His drawings too were dark and twisted, an expression of the chronic anxiety with which he was diagnosed. I'd heard he'd been a bank robber, which made a kind of sense as I guess he'd lived off his nerves and they had finally broken. "It's me nerves," was his refrain. Sometimes he would leap up and try to lay the tables ready for mealtimes, even though they were over an hour away. He tried, unsuccessfully, to hang himself one day from the railing around his hospital bed with a pair of socks, but being so tall his feet had still been able to reach the ground and then the whole railing had collapsed. Eventually he was given ECT and it worked miraculously. Within a day or so he was wandering around, relaxed and cheerful, joking with staff and patients. When his family came in to collect him he shook me heartily by the hand and thanked me for my kindness. A few months later he was back again, tying himself in knots.

One day in midsummer I remember walking into the ward and seeing a man with a shock of curly brown hair sitting topless by an open window, with wasps crawling over his puffy white arms and torso. His watery eyes were staring into space and he hardly noticed me enter the dormitory. When I talked to him it turned out he was a medium with the Spiritualist Church not far up the road, and his son and daughter had had him admitted for *hearing voices*.

"I've always heard voices," he said, adding that his wife had died and that they were after his house.

I still wonder whether what he told me was true. If so, it was truly horrible.

It was around this time that things began to take a downward spiral for me. I had a readmitted patient who suffered, like his wife, from mental health issues and alcoholism. They had made a suicide pact, taking pills and whisky and then putting carrier bags over their heads. It was his job to secure the bags. Unfortunately, after securing his wife's, he'd passed out and been woken by the police to find her dead beside him. It had been Christmas and I'd just returned to work. The patient lived in the same road as me. The next day I arrived to find that he had escaped and jumped from the multi-storey car park. It was too much to bear. Shortly afterwards I woke in my friend Mr Alan's room and realised

I wouldn't return to the brick-built Victorian asylum up on the hill. Despite the pain I felt, and still feel, it altered me for the better, teaching me what it means to be human. It sculpted me into who I am, both as an entity and an artist.

I remember being asked to take a patient back to his ward. They had referred him to Occupational Therapy because, although he refused to walk, feed, toilet himself or speak, there was apparently nothing physically wrong with him. As I wheeled him along the corridors a silence steadily settled in. When I'd tried to engage him in my usual *jolly* conversation on the journey to the group, I'd been aware of his gaze upon me. There seemed to be a malevolence about it that unnerved me. Now, in the silent deserted corridors, scattered with the odd shoe or chocolate wrapper, I began to feel the fear rising within me. He hated my positivity and joy. It repulsed him, like the rest of the human race. He had retreated inside his own body. At the same time I felt like I understood it, it was like *fugue syndrome*, running away, but not physically deserting a place, running into one's own interior. I felt like I was walking deeper into the corridors of his mind, toward a centre where I might find him there waiting for me. In his grief he had deserted the exterior world, vowing never to emerge. This was a dark journey.

Years later I found myself filming Pat Higgins' *KillerKiller* at the hospital, which was being rebuilt into luxury flats. As we were shooting a scene, the sound man suddenly waved at us to stop, and we all heard footsteps approaching the door at the end of the corridor. Pat said "Cut," and shouted out to the person the other side. "We're in the middle of a take!" No reply. We waited. Nothing. Pat walked to the door and opened it. There was no one there. He walked along the corridor beyond and eventually came back, pasty-faced. "No one there," he said, "but you all heard the footsteps, right?" We had. Perhaps amidst the forgotten cardboard document wallets and scrawls of graffiti, beneath the peeling honeycomb ceilings and the odd item of dusty clothing, walked the souls of those who had dwelt there, those for whom it had been a sanctuary from the world outside.

—— *Sue* ——

The girl is finishing her work day breakfast. It's another early morning, and quite a bright one, so from the fifteenth floor of the East End tower block the view isn't as grey as it can be. There's a window all along one wall but the balcony's closed off in case of jumpers. It's been a few weeks since she moved into this flat but she's still in love with it. It's her adventure. The under floor heating feels good under her bare feet, and so does she. She always does. Even on a Thursday when they've been clubbing through to the middle of the night she wakes excited, optimistic, prepared.

Teaching is what she does best, what she loves, an act of faith because she's not afraid of the challenges, of labels like Educational Priority Area, of urban wastelands Mum can only guess. She chose it all, to do the best she can where it counts, so she doesn't mind weekends on the floor making work-cards in felt-tipped colour, sealed in sticky-back plastic, or the research, cutting and sticking. She loves the kids, just about all of them. But it's instinct that makes the difference. She's no good at anything that doesn't come naturally, and the classroom is where she's most instinctive. Not a nightclub, even with her new body and the freshly hennaed curls that earn her compliments from men who dance with her and want her number – unaware that she may be the only twenty-two-year-old virgin in London. Not on the phone to Mum, who worried even before a crate of empty milk bottles dropped from a height to land at her feet when she visited. Even though that day there was no urine, dirty mattress or blood in the lift.

"I love it here," she defended. "It's real." And she does, apart from the echoing corridors like underground tunnels with doors people hide behind, and the days when the lift's out of order and she has a few hundred steps to climb with books to mark.

She's watching the time now, thinking about the first lesson, how the topic she planned is taking shape, and ways to refuse offers of lifts from the Deputy Head who is meant to be a *wolf* with a grin to match. While her flatmate sings in the bathroom, she applies mascara. The doorbell rings. She goes to answer, guessing it's a parcel. As she opens the door, it's thrust back at her and a tall, thin man barges in. He shuts the door behind him and looks at her as if he can't process what he's seeing but doesn't like it anyway. Unable to move or speak, she leans against the wall. She doesn't even think her friend has heard what's happened over running water and her own version of *She's the Greatest Dancer*.

"It's all right," he says. "I won't hurt you. I'm just on the run from the police."

He's young, but older than her. His hair is long and uncombed; his shirt is floral and loose over his jeans. The girl has no idea what to say. Will it make any difference if she explains that they're going to work soon? In her head there are nightmares, film trailers for movies she would never want to see, news stories. And BT hasn't installed their phone line yet.

Then her flatmate emerges from the bathroom with crinkly wet hair, her pink robe tied tightly around her waist. Her face is rosy from her shower but she doesn't look horrified or even surprised.

She tells him their names and asks, "And you're ...?"

Ignoring the question and the introductions too, he repeats that he won't hurt anyone but needs a place to hide.

"The thing is," her flatmate tells him, "we'd like to chat but we're teachers and we have to get ready for work and I'm dripping. So I need to get the hairdryer now."

And she goes. The girl waits silently, still pressed to the wall as if it will give way and let her out of her dream into the world she recognises. He edges further in, talking about the police and how they're after him. There's no sign of any weapon on his lean body.

Returning with the hairdryer, her friend turns it on, and stands there, talking over it. Shorter and curvier than the girl, and sexier, she smells of sweet citrus. She has a louder laugh and smarter banter. She reckons sixteen-year-old lads respect her and the girl has no reason to doubt it. She asks him where he lives, where his mum is and whether he needs a glass of water.

He doesn't answer, shakes his head. The girl hasn't spoken. She doesn't know how much time has passed. She's never been late for anything.

"Come to tea on Sunday," her flatmate suggests, smiling. She grew up in the Methodist church. "I'll make a cake. Bring your mum. But now isn't good timing."

The girl is awestruck, astonished. She knows she's useless, immobilised. Still talking, her friend tells him she's getting dressed now but he can help himself to food in the kitchen. He hesitates, but moves towards it, looking on both sides of the door as if Dennis Waterman and John Thaw are about to jump out and tell him he's nicked.

Her flatmate is dressed before he comes back chewing a slice of bread.

"All right," she says, "we have to leave now."

His head is shaking.

"Come on. Time to go."

"No."

"If you won't go, my friend will have to go and call the police."

The girl stares. She can't leave her alone with him. But however nicely and firmly he's asked, he doesn't move.

She hears, "She's going now. You know what's best. No one wants to get you into trouble."

He's agitated but nothing gets through. All he does is look nervously around the flat as if a boyfriend with a six-pack might be under the covers in her friend's room. Not hers.

"She's going to make that call now."

The girl knows what she's supposed to do. Looking back anxiously, she walks out of the flat, imagining his arm blocking her, his hand to her throat. But he doesn't try to stop her. There's a door opposite but she's no idea who lives there. She knocks loudly, repeatedly. No answer. No answer at the next door. At the third, a man opens and she cries, "Please, I need to call the police. There's an intruder in our flat and my friend's in there with him." Frowning, he shuts the door on her, and she's crying now. Her face is burning with the tears and her throat feels as if there's no air in this corridor. She runs to the next flat and the woman there seems suspicious, but lets her in to make the call. Only she knows it could be too late. She tries to be clear, waste no words, give the facts fast.

Coming out onto the corridor she hears the lift go down. Their door is open now and her flatmate calls her name, asking if she's all right before she tells her he's gone. They hug. The girl is shaking. She's told to sit down. It's as if she's been ill. But now they have to wait for the police and there's no way of telling the two school offices why they won't be there for nine o'clock.

Offered coffee, the girl insists she will make it. Again and again she apologises for being helpless. It's shocking her now, the memory of the ice sculpture she became, as if all she could do was wait for a magic spell to break her free. She says how grateful she is, and asks whether her friend was planning to use the hairdryer as a weapon if she had to.

"Too right! Wallop!"

They laugh about the invitation to Sunday tea.

"I don't think he's dangerous," her flatmate says.

The girl agrees. She feels sorry for him in a way. But what if he comes back?

When an overweight policeman arrives, moving too slowly to catch any eight-year-old in the girl's class, he knows who they mean and tells them he's *probably harmless*, a victim of Care in the Community, a druggie, mostly off his head. Still, he says they must be in shock and tells them to be more careful. Why on earth did they open the door without knowing who was there?

The girl flushes; she doesn't know. It was one of many things she was brought up not to do. She feels as if she's lived twenty-two years for nothing.

Her friend tells her the thing to do is learn from it. She'll call BT. They'll buy a chain and spy-hole. The girl decides they need a whistle too, an Acme Thunderer, and that evening she hangs it beside the door on a thread of wool.

Three days later when the doorbell rings at the same time, she hurries to the door, crouches down to the letterbox and sees his mouth.

He whispers, "It's me."

She frees the whistle from its hook, positions herself and blows hard. He runs, and he doesn't come back.

It'll be a story, but not one Mum and Dad will ever hear.

—— *Leslie* ——

I went through a stage of being fascinated by my own appearance. I'd lock the bathroom door and stare into the mirror, silently mouthing words like *lovely* and *beautiful*. I knew it was wrong, but I rationalised it as a deliberate experiment that I'd soon grow out of. When my mirror-play became a habit, I told myself it wasn't important, or real even, and that what was happening was just a form of theatre. The nice-looking face I could see was my creation, a mysterious being who only existed through my say-so because I was the artist who brought her to life.

My self-obsession began earlier, while taking long baths. To lie there at ease with my body on show was a floaty experience. I was absorbed into something smooth and seamless and gently physical; I'd become my own admirer. And yet I was full of impossible hopes and wishes. I was a dreamer; my life was imperfect; my body wasn't what it should be.

Much later, overcoming my embarrassment, I began to analyse my obsession. I wrote about it in a poem, using third person to probe my own experience. What had seemed shameful at the time now looked like a defensive formulation. There was a disconnection about it, a gap between me and my image. At the same time it had set me apart and made me feel special. In the bath, I'd come alive. Even if my identity wasn't clear, at least I'd found a place where I could be *someone*.

Still later, building on my poem, I wrote this story:

There's a boy I can see, soaking in the bath. I notice his pink, blotchy skin and photographic smile. In his face I can read things – pipe-dreams and wishes, filling up his head. For now he's holding his breath, preparing to go under. When he pops back up, he pictures himself as a mermaid basking on rocks. At least, that's what he's thinking. Of course he knows it's not true, but he likes his stories. There's a craziness about them, a liberty taken. In them, he can be anyone.

The tiles in the bathroom are running steam. The mirror's wet too. A mist haze hangs around the ceiling like smoke. The room's warm and sweaty.

Something strange is happening. His old self is dissolving like soap in water, leaving him behind. It's all down the overflow and out of sight. What's left is something hard to reach – he's colourless, odourless, a soft-boy in water.

So where is he now? In his mind he's on the beach, hearing the waves. Now he's in the tent changing with his mother, and running out to sea. The wind's getting up, she's one step ahead, and he's calling, "Wait for me!"

She stops and takes off her bathing cap, shaking out her hair. It's loose around her face and one strand catches in her mouth. His thoughts flash back to the dunes, chewing on grass, and he blushes slightly – but then she tucks her cap back on and they're running into water.

"Cold!" he cries and wades in slowly, holding his breath. His foot catches on something hard and he sees himself blue-faced and hopping, caught by a crab. Although he knows it's silly, the thought makes him shaky. His left leg is stick-thin, encased in plaster. The pain and the fear keep him struggling until, pulling himself up, he spreads his arms and pushes on. As the water gets deeper the waves take over; they're stronger than he thought. When he stops they become soft ice, clamped around his waist. In front of him now he can see his mother's head bobbing like a cork. "Come in deep, it's lovely!" she calls, waving, but he's stuck to the bottom, all puffed out. The water's getting higher, up to his chest – and now his body's fading, the steam's all around, and he's lying in the bath.

So how did he get here, he wonders, and what has he become? Is it that the water has touched him and changed him – like baptism, perhaps? Or could he be in-between and different; something like a girl? That would be nice. Boy to girl, with silk-smooth body, and no one looking. It should be simple. He's peering down *there* and tucking in his *thing*, squeezed back with the rest, like grapes. He's woman-smooth and beautiful: Adonis in the bath.

    Hey worm.
    Worm?
    Look at me.
    Me?
    LOOK AT ME.
    Yes.
    Don't look away.
    All right.
    Now say sorry.
    Sorry?
    SAY SORRY.
    Sorry.
    MEAN IT. Say *Sorry.*
    Sorry.
    Sorry lord and master.
    Sorry lord and master.
    Sorry your highness.
    Sorry your highness.
    Sorry Almighty One.
    What?
    Cheek —

The bathroom's locked and he's on the inside. It's a slow backwater where he can dream and be free; it's his place of rest. In here he's a ship floating out, turning on the tide. Or could he be the hand that breaks the surface, the forgotten swimmer crossing the water? If he is, he's also a child at the edge of the swimming pool. The ladder's in his hand and he's taking in air. Soon he'll let go. He's Ophelia drifting; the Lady of the Lake.

    As he sinks to the bottom his arms go up and he sees himself drowning. A beautiful boy, if it wasn't for *that.* All that flesh. The ugly stuff with dewlap and wrinkles. The dirt and soreness. The dribble in the pants.

But he's put that all away. He's up to the neck, pink and blotchy, soaking in the bath.

And now he's on the floor. He's the paper-bag kid dumped in the corner, who no one wants to know. There's a stillness around him, a closed-up shell. And inside, he's hearing them calling out, "Ad-on-is, Ad-on-is. Ad-on-is a girl."

The bully wants to finish him. He's landing his blows and enjoying what he does. There are other boys with him, looking for action. They're grinning too.

"Ad-on-is, Ad-on-is. Ad-on-is a girl."

The punching stops; the bully walks away. With his nose streaming blood, the kid gets up.

When the water strikes flesh, the splashes are cold. The waves take over. Their power comes from somewhere deep. Each one is a heartbeat. They take away her breath.

1.

As a boy, I dreamed about wars. I fantasised journeys into darkness and heroic struggles leading to chases and underground escapes. Walking down the street, I was in action, dodging bullets and overleaping walls, and when I got home I was in my bunker, studying my maps and planning my campaign. In my head I was playing what diplomats called *The Great Game*. What would have happened, I asked myself, if Napoleon had conquered Russia or Hitler had won the Battle of the Bulge? The answer, of course, was all about me, or my secret-agent-self code named   . I could picture myself as an unsung hero leading the resistance in occupied London, and I was there, unseen, at El Alamein and Waterloo.

In my dreams of war there were no final victories, just short-lived stand-offs before the next battle. No winners, no losers, and no deaths either. Instead there were miraculous escapes and sudden disappearances and comeback campaigns where I switched sides at will from conquering hero to scheming prisoner dreaming his escape.

So why did I do it?

My war studies were an attempt to control the world, working out my moves like a chess player. It was my way of achieving the impossible, and it went with my interest in telekinesis and space exploration. Pure thought had its own territory, a world of otherness where the restrictions of life were lifted for a moment and the perspective changed. But although my wars were mental, they were also quite immediate. Carried out to the tune of *Jerusalem*, they were closely-fought struggles between evenly matched sides where the outcome hung in the balance – and, as in sport, the result might hinge on a single mistake. So I walked down the street choosing my route and channelling my thoughts in just the right direction. I was a warrior on high alert: one false step and the enemy might win. My task was evasion. So I lectured myself to watch my back and cover all angles; I looked ahead and spotted dangers; I approached each corner expecting an attack.

The boys at school understood war differently. They thought fighting was fun; they did it because it brought them alive. Dancing like boxers, they punched the air and sprayed each other with bullets.

"Drrrrrrrrrrrr," shouted Jack, as if he was drilling into rock.

"Ratatatatat," replied Barry.

"Splat-splat-splat," called George, diving behind a wall.

At other times they played prisoners and jailers. They were the tough nuts, the ones with *front* who got their own way. So they'd tread on someone's toes or pull a lock of hair, or grab what they shouldn't – and afterwards punish wrongdoers using glue and matches.

Much later, I wrote a poem about childhood that included the boys. They came in after the words *singing to family*.

The boys sang it different. *One in a taxi one in a car ...*
Ta ra ra boom te ay, as chipmunks. Then Colonel Bogey.

One did the bear walk, right sock up, left sock down.
He used the words.

One played boffin,
deaf man talking, he came from Mars.

One showed muscle. Fingers in armpits,
Ugh ugh, King Kong.

Their leader trained beetles.
His shirt hid burn marks,
he exposed them to the girls.

They all did the boss. Then stuck it with bubblegum.

Get it? they jawed, talking yaarish
as they pushed from behind.
Yuh? was deadpan, *Yuh, yuh* might hurt.

Upstairs, off-key, back of the bus,
they murdered John Brown,
then did time on go-slow
prospecting in inkwells to freshen up their nibs.

Cross-eyed at will, they drew with ease,
could cartwheel, swim, yodel,
rode backwards one-handed,
caught balls against the sun, knew how to lie.

One used a penknife, one exploded bangers,
two collected from the poor.

Experts, they performed on yo-yos,
whistled tunes in chorus, beat time with fists.

Then set up little traps: passwords, permissions,
war zones with lookouts
for ambush and sentencing
and houses of correction.

Or, shaking off the drops,

hummed *The German Officer* quickly glancing down
then, nose up to whiteness, stared straight ahead
awed by the size
of some imaginary schoolboy deity.

2.

I'm looking at photos of me from the past. They're black and white and wavy around the edges with a grey film behind, as if they'd been taken underwater. I touch them lightly, turning over the pages. They belong to a different world, a still-life story in which I'm someone else: a short-haired boy wearing sandals, surrounded by family. The grandparents are there, alive but blurry, pictured in party hats in front of flock wallpaper – and in the next frame, in overcoats and deck chairs, sitting on the beach. In other pictures they're out walking in what looks like a faint mist. It's grey and cloudy and everyone's wearing patterned, hand-knitted jumpers and corduroy trousers. Where the group takes up a pose I'm at the front, a child on my own, gap-toothed and grinning.

Looking at those pictures is quite different from the life they represented. In the photos there's a boy whose body shape changes from skinny-in-trunks to flabby pre-teen. His face, too, shifts from thin and weathered to slightly puffy. He's a self-absorbed child, then boy mark one, then boy mark two, and in each variation he's smiling shyly, playing nice-boy to the camera.

But the pictures are part of a dead world. It's cold and shivery in there, and empty. I've passed through the mirror, like Alice, and I'm tiptoeing over carpet in an upstairs room. There are TV noises from below and intermittent voices – in my memory they fill up the house with invisible watchers: strange otherworldly presences that hid in corners and appeared at night, imitating my parents. They were dangerous, of course, lurking in wardrobes and concealed behind mirrors, and could take over the house in the blink of an eye.

And the pictures kept coming. Topsy-turvy adventures as I crawled up cliffs and abseiled between rocks, followed by a rope snapping and drop to the bottom. Each time, my fall ends in a cell with spikes descending from the ceiling. It's dark, and I'm in the cinema, hoping for a breakout – although I know it won't happen till next week's episode. In the meantime I imagine Houdini-like escapes. I upend a stone to block the spikes while I tunnel through the floor. Or I crouch beneath the table, and when that splinters take refuge by the door. Or I climb up to the windowsill and thin myself to nothing.

I can still see the pictures of my weekly disappearance. It's a dream sequence where I pass through cracks like water and walk up walls. My parents are around but I'm upstairs, in my own walkie-talkie space, plotting my Great Escape. I'm in shadow, invisible even to myself, with nothing to show except my own madcap thoughts.

I can hear them now, as I write ...

Oh no, you didn't-didn't-didn't do that, did you – *did you*?

See those boys? No, not scared. Turn the other cheek. Pretender.

Won't go away. Lie down, go quiet. Just don't.

Stupid, you are. Unlucky you is. Stupid-stupid.

I didn't say that. I didn't. I DID NOT SAY THAT.

But none of this shows in the photographs.

3.

The new boy was nine when he joined Stoneway School. Tall for his age, there was an attentive softness about him, a smooth-faced gentleness that made him seem rather un-boyish. He was slim rather than muscly, chatty not shouty, and he moved loosely, in his own indeterminate space, so you might think he was absent. He smiled when he sat down, as if he was on stage – and kept on smiling in a look-at-me way as he tucked himself in.

But being smiley wasn't all good. There was a lack of definition in his gentleness; it made him standoffish and not quite there. To his classmates he was odd: a wrong 'un, a boy to be laughed at or avoided.

When the teacher called his name, the lads at the back exchanged glances.

"You're *Joseph*?" one of them asked at play time.

The new boy nodded.

His questioner scowled. "You Jo-Jo?" he went on, angling his jaw forward.

Joseph gave a shrug, and smiled.

"You know who I am?"

Joseph's mouth opened; his smile was fading. But before he could answer another boy stepped forward. "That's Hardnut Clive," he said.

In the silence that followed Clive came closer. He had hairs on his chin and a pimply, scrunched-up face. "Hey you, Josephine," he whispered gently, then called out sharply raising his arm. "Hey, Dozy Josie. It's you I'm talking to." Behind him two other lads were standing grinning, with their hands in their pockets. Suddenly Hardnut stepped back, cupping one hand to his mouth as he shouted to the world, "Jo-Jo – Josie – Josephine! Jo-Jo – Josie – Josephine!" He continued yelling and hooting as he strode around the playground, jabbing his forefinger at his target and rolling his eyes till the bell rang for class.

There were other names, too. *Weirdo* was one, given to him by Coco – aka Harry – because he walked like a girl, *Queer* was another and *Girlie*, both Clive's – but mainly he was *Joseph-ine*, with the last syllable added silently by the listeners who narrowed their eyes and bunched their fists whenever they saw him.

With the girls it was different. When Joe walked in he felt a connection. Girls belonged to story books and quiet moments. When you were near them it was like standing in sunlight and being called by name. They were all eyes and ears, but unlike the boys they played it down, making him welcome without too much fuss. Whoever he was, they were willing to wait.

Not that they had to. Because on his arrival Joe was told by the teacher to sit with the girls.

"Just for now," she said. "The boys' tables are full."

And she steered him to a place by the window, leaving him with three shiny-faced girls who stopped what they were doing to ask him questions. Each had a green name band around her wrist. Amie spoke first, with Clare and Lucy acting as chorus, asking his name, his favourite colour, what animals he liked, lessons he was good at and foods he hated – listening to his answers with slightly pushy smiles. From then on Joe sat at their table accepting their attentions and learning how they did things. Because Amie, Clare and Lucy were the kind of girls who the boys called *goodie goodies* – they did what they were asked, talked behind their hands and smiled all-innocence when the teacher asked questions.

Playing outside was another story. Amie, Clare and Lucy were top runners: the kind of super-fast girls who led the sports team and could chase down rivals. And when it came to tag if Clare and Lucy were speedy, Amie was the speediest. As *it* she could overtake anybody, adding them to the chain and swinging them around until they were dizzy.

When it happened to Joe, he went with it. To be lifted and spun made him feel strong and special and Peter Pan-ish. He was alive and weightless, he could fly, and when the ground came up to meet him he laughed.

But the bump really hurt. And afterwards his head was full of flashing lights.

It was Amie who spoke first.

"You're fast," she said, touching his hair.

Joe shivered. Beneath him, the ground was still moving.

"Very fast," put in Clare, smiling.

"Boy you're super-fast," added Lucy, and she eyed him like a prize animal.

For Joe it was like being inside a closed room, on the wrong side of glass. A stiffness had taken over, the girls were watching, and he was out of breath.

That afternoon in class Amie played footsie, tapping rhythms on Joe's ankle. He allowed it, pretending it wasn't happening. No one seemed to notice, and at home time, except for one quick glance, there was nothing to show. The next day was the same, with a wink and a few more glances. In the week that followed she went further, treading on his toes and elbowing him in queues, then half-tripping him as they went outside. Joe, she announced, could be annoying. He was at fault for nudging her when her pen went astray; he lost her books, broke her pencils, and when water spilt down her front it was all because of Joe-Joe.

"Stop hurting!" she cried, later in the playground when Clumsy-Joe's fingers caught in her hair.

That was when she hit him. Not hard but glancingly, hand on cheek, turning to a stroke.

When Clare and Lucy saw, they said things.

"He's not yours to play with," called Clare.

"Yes he is. We're besties," replied Amie.

"No. Not yours. Not Clare's," put in Lucy. "Just mine."

"He's mine."

"Mine!"

"Mine!"

Suddenly, finding himself surrounded, Joe windmilled his arms. "Not yours!" he shouted, pushing free.

He set off, still shouting, with the girls behind him. Knowing that they'd catch him, he headed for the gate. As he ran, his cry went up, echoing and repeating like a bird. It rang inside his head as if he was hearing the end-of-playtime bell. He was crying now as he reached the fence. "No!" he yelled, when Amie caught his arm. As he shook himself free he stumbled and the fence came up to meet him.

The next day when class began, the table where Joe and the three girls sat had been cleared. Four chairs had been tucked underneath. The thick, protective tablecloth had been removed exposing paint-stained wood. There were strange animal shapes and initials scratched into the surface. In the centre was a pile of green, Egyptian-style wristbands. They were coiled around each other like snakes. The names on the wristbands read Amie, Clare, Lucy and Jo.

4.

I was the girl I fell for. I knew it was wrong of me and stupid. That's why I looked away when I saw her in the mirror. What do you say to a girl anyway who doesn't know you're there? The sad-and-deep type who turns her head and walks off at the end of the story? The nose-in-the-air old-fashioned sort wearing shiny shoes and hairbands? The girl letting down her hair to stand wide-eyed at the window – or the other girl hidden in the wardrobe and the underwear drawer?

My girl knew, of course. I could feel her blush growing inside me. She gave me her hand and my nails grew long. Her unseen shined-up skin was mine – hairless, mostly, and smooth where it mattered. No curves as such but soft around the mouth – with a head-to-heart connection like a rose on a stem.

I kept my girl secret. Her voice spoke quietly in my head. No one saw her, or suspected she was there. She was the Ice Queen, the siren, the teaser in the mirror.

And that's where we kissed.

—— Cy ——

The Pissed Family Slobinson was my private name for those souls who found themselves marooned on the bohemian island of madness that was the house Sam and I rented after university. Together with our director Paul Battin and writer friend Leigh we were more often known as *The Ash Gang* on account of our Ashford Avenue address, but also the amount of 'ashish which was inhaled within those nicotine-stained walls. What I chiefly remember was the scarred and pitted wooden surface of the large dining table. It was stuck with multi-coloured detritus like the skin of a sperm whale surfacing through a sea of alcohol. On many nights the table had been a roof over my head as I slowly sank down, finally slipping from my chair to wake up at exactly 2 a.m. wondering if our friend Hilary had left a half-drunk bottle of white wine chilling in the fridge for my breakfast. The kitchen diner was to me like the time-locked bridge of an airship galleon, steered by dreams and fuelled by narcotics and Bikini Rum. Solitary strip drinking became a favourite game of mine and I'd often be found lying on the breakfast bar in various states of undress with my head between the speakers of the stereo listening to Vivaldi's *Four Seasons* or *The Planets* suite. I drank a lot and ate very little – but would occasionally feast, anaconda-like, on something called a Mega-pie with my shipmates. In my mind the pie itself was like a round table and we would carve it up with swords and out of it would leap the rest of the Knights.

I remember one morning, having fallen asleep in sunshine after a solitary Karaoke session to *Kashmir* by Led Zeppelin, wandering indoors to search for more left-over booze and making a mandala on the table out of matchsticks, with my Buddha at its centre. In each segment I

placed a piece of the debris I found littering the house. Bits of various coloured Rizla and crisp packets, torn train tickets, foil balls and chocolate bar wrappers, ring-pulls, pen lids, pistachio shells. It was a thing of beauty.
At night, the kitchen, which lay beyond the breakfast bar, became a nightclub dance floor. I can picture myself as Biff, The Amazing Mahogany Boy with Roach, The Magic Whisky Boy raving, wild-eyed to The Prodigy. Meanwhile, the table was a hive of industry. Fingers rolled an impressive origami selection of spliffs, shaped like carrots or trumpets or horizontal skyscrapers. This was an ancient magic happening; one similar to tribes telling stories that far surpassed the boundaries of logical thinking. We wove words and ideas into multi-coloured and layered structures, connecting us with the universe and with our whole selves.
One morning as the sun rose I watched Mr Alan, who often joined us there, squatting beneath the tree in the back garden. As the dawn chorus climaxed, he was transformed into an eagle-beaked beast. His feet became roots that snaked into the earth, entwining with the mycelium. **He seemed at one with nature: part-bird, part-plant and somehow both human** and fungi. To me, with his long hair and dark, penetrating gaze, it was as if he could see through the fabric of reality.
The night before Mr Alan and I had gone on a quest for Roach's Magic Whisky to The Soupmaker's house. We had walked through a railway tunnel, finding ourselves trapped in a time loop. As if walking on a treadmill we met each other's eyes and the tunnel walls streamed past, it seemed forever, his hair blowing backwards as we moved onwards but stood still.
Inside, the house had a living room, a hall and a kitchen. But we were lost. We wandered in what seemed like a mirrored labyrinth. It was as if MC Escher had redesigned the interior and I half expected that we would

look up and see scientists removing the roof and charting our progress to the goal, The Magic Whisky. After what felt like days we met in the hallway with Mr Alan clutching the bottle firmly in his hand. We looked at each other, both realising what had happened, and bolted for the front door. We'd made it. But I think we both retained the knowledge that we had experienced a Night Sea Journey within our own minds.

We were *wired to the moon* of course as Mr Alan always said. On our return Mr Alan had climbed up onto the roof of the house, and as I clambered out of a bedroom window to join him he pointed to the night sky. "Do you see that?" There was a giant question mark made out of stars in the sky.

What I experienced at these times was a pure clarity of vision. I felt more like myself, more whole. And out of the stories with characters and the games played flowed a reservoir of material for *Sam and Cy* comedy. Ashford Avenue pulsed with creativity. There was poetry and live music, dancers and painters, writers, singers, actors and of course comedians. But, above all, there were our adventures. One night returning from the pub, as Paul played a Victorian adventurer beating down the undergrowth with an umbrella, Sam fell into a hole and sprained his ankle. Filled with superhuman strength, I lifted him and carried him on my back as if I were his steed. As the others leapt across a wide stream I stopped. The gap seemed too far even for me to jump. "Come on! You're as strong as an ox, man!" shouted Sam. Backing up I charged, almost making it before we both tumbled back into the water, Sam beneath me, squashed in the mud.

On another occasion I remember the two of us in a Dionysian frenzy of summer joy stripping naked and running out into the night. As the security light at the back of the house switched on, the rest of the party watched us through the window as if it was a cinema screen. We ran and bounced through the shrubbery until finally we hit the nettle patch. There we leapt high into the air, caterwauling. This incident, and its ensuing hilarity, was burnt into our feet and our memories for a long time afterwards.

One morning I woke up, lost in darkness. Moving slowly, I groped around the room but nothing seemed familiar. Eventually I found a door handle and light streamed in to reveal Mr Alan lying on the bed fully clothed. I had obviously collapsed on his floor. With the light came memories of Irish Whisky and LSD from the night before. I felt good. Leaving the house, I saw commuters, shoppers, the sun steaming down, but in a very different way. The veil had been lifted. As I cut through a copse on the way back to Ashford Avenue, the world transformed from concrete and brick into thick foliage and the sound of birdsong. Reaching a break in the trees, I looked at the Victorian asylum on the hill. Pulling a cigarette out of the crumpled packet in my jeans pocket, I stared across the valley at the hospital.

I knew in that moment that I was looking into the past. The redbrick chimneys of the Victorian asylum were no longer my present. My work there was done and I couldn't go back. The Ashford Avenue days were also time-locked – sealed in a loop. Sam had left, and the walls of the house were crumbling. For me at least, darkness had crept into our gatherings, and the wild days of infinite summer were being drained of light. That light would be rekindled on many occasions, but for now Ashford Avenue had become an idea, a lost moment outside time to be reawakened in the mind whenever two or more of us met. It was only in its beginnings that it required a real and actual basis.

FINDING A PATH

―― *Leslie* ――

We're walking in the woods. It's just Sue and me. We're husband and wife, walking in a pool of calm. It's like being inside a clear glass jar, or underwater. There are sounds, of course – a plane overhead, our own breath, occasional birdsong – but they come to us through a wall of silence. The shapes, too, are at one remove, like sketches in an empty gallery. So we walk through sunlight and shade with the leaves and branches looking like cut-outs.

On our walk there are rest stops. Places where we shelter in half-light, or listen to the rain. They are spots to fall back on or look forward to, making us think of childhood hideouts and imaginary journeys. Inside their protection we're actors in a quietly-told story where nothing much happens. We stand listening, hand in hand. It's like watching water – underneath everything's moving while the surface stays clear and still. And although we're at the centre, the life we experience is shifting, big-screen and out there beyond us.

When Sue and I are asked as authors about where our ideas come from, we often mention walking in the woods. We describe how we use our rambles to discuss an idea, or talk through a character. It's a chance, we say, to share the difficulties and think about where we're going. What we don't mention is how writing can go off on a tack, losing direction like a slow walk, or how we come across places where almost any route is possible. The parallels go further. In the woods the light is partial, so ordinary details may blur and take on shapes that seem unfamiliar. Sometimes it's as if we're walking through memory guided only by our feelings, and the things we see are full of special significance. Our task, it seems, is to watch and listen without imposing anything. We're in the flow, observing and taking notes, while going in deep.

But the two experiences are rather different. Because writing is an OCD habit combining close-up observation with a clear sense of direction. So the author in me is constantly stopping to listen and re-jig the words, whereas walking together is freeform and unconscious. We're simply letting go – although that, too, requires directed attention. There's an adjustment to be made, and we make it, moving from busy-busy to drift and flow. We could be walking through dreams or standing on the beach looking out to sea when it's windless ...

—— *Sue* ——

Leslie: What happens when you write and where does your facility come from?
Sue: I start with an idea, which is usually a character in a particular situation. I sometimes get close to that character through a diagram, but sometimes I feel as if I already know that character intuitively and just start. If a story turns out to be plot-heavy, I often stop two thirds of the way in to try to make sure I know where each thread will go and the weave all fits to-

gether. Mostly, though, there's no plot until the characters direct developments without much interference from me.

As for my facility, I began to write stories at the age of five and told them before that, so it's been a lifelong habit that's become my identity, but the encouragement I received, from my father and teachers, was crucial in making me believe that writing was what I did best. My family valued stories. They were seen as a joy but also as important sources of a deeper truth.

—— *Leslie* ——

I sometimes see woods when I'm falling asleep. It's a good sign when I do. It happens usually after I've been absorbed in something low-key and aimless. The trees I see are grey, and frame the path like doorways. They draw me into where the world softens, blurring the line between mind and body. So I'm experiencing a kind of back-lit, unreal journey where picture and observer are both in flux. At the same time I'm aware of my own mind shaping the story. But it could be me inside someone else, dreaming who I am. So it's a blank screen trip where anything might happen.

Sometimes as I fall asleep, I've a feeling that Sue's by me and we're in a bubble of light. But whereas our walks are physical and sensual, this feels disembodied. There's an aura around us, a mist-dream of thought. It suggests, for a moment, the *invisiblist* fantasies of childhood. And as I drop off, I'm happy and floaty and not alone. We're in the woods, walking in silence, as the light begins to fade ...

I wrote a poem describing our wood walks. It's about the power of the imagination.

In Medias Res

Uphill, circling through elder and oak
we follow the path,
one side open with stud fields and farms,
the other hollowed into dark.

Somewhere out there I'm on a drive,
on early morning map search, visiting a school.
You're there by me, in author dress and tights.

We're crossing between lives,
finding ourselves, this dark-light moment,
on the way to what is real.

Arriving, we unload. After signing in,
we pass through doors
to a soft-floored, bright-walled, star-lined classroom
where you take them on a journey.

Greetings. The ideas flow.
Quiz show and answers. Their guesses are good.

And now, between tree root and shadow,
our path leads back,
side by side and looking both ways,
and filling up the air with quickness.

We're here and somewhere else.
Brightside and the ditch.

In both, we're present tense.

So, what about the back story to our walk and how did we get to the woods?

Sue and I left the house early, passing through empty streets to reach the trees where we sidestepped bushes and skirted logs, talking about writing as we walked. We were inside the bubble, in a bedroom, or on the road to visit a school; we were dreaming or remembering the stories of hauntings and being on the run. And our walk went on through light and shade and roots and branches and feather-veined leaves, arriving finally, at silence and standstill. And there we'd reached what we thought of as a maze. In fact, we'd been walking, that was all. Nothing had changed, except in our heads. But of course the mind is everything ...

—— *Sue* ——

Leslie: You believe in the power of stories. In your life, how have you experienced that power?

Sue: Stories have always held me in their power, which feels greatest when they reduce me to tears or invade my reality so vividly that I can't shake them off when I've set the book aside. I feel great empathy when I read fiction, and when I'm writing it the connection between me and my characters feels even stronger and deeper. It's true that when I wrote *The Waterhouse Girl*, about a character with alopecia, it changed my life. Firstly, the cathartic process of channelling my own experience into a novel that had its own shape and life began to make me look at hair loss differently. I realised that I wanted to be as brave and compassionate as Daisy Waterhouse – and to stop feeling so undermined by my baldness. Secondly, it made me an author, because it gave me a story that hadn't been told before and one I could write with authentic detail and intensity, and because Michael Morpurgo's praise for my manuscript gave me a new faith and resilience. If he believed I was a good writer, I mustn't give up hope. Then, once published, my story encouraged many readers with alopecia. I remember the first time I realised its impact out there in the world. A teacher, whose daughter had lost her hair at the age of eight, said, "I just want to say thank you. We read it together every night and it made such a difference." But the most striking evidence of the power of stories has to be the Y8 boy who told me, "You made me a better person" – because that novel helped him to understand how hard it must be to be different, and that changed his attitudes and behaviour. Stories can change us!

Leslie

There were bodies in the woods. Everyone knew it. It was said they were German soldiers who'd parachuted in. People had different theories about how they died. In some versions they'd been there for years living on berries and roots but had surrendered when they'd fallen ill. In this story they'd become bent-backed and trollish, shuffling sideways and speaking in grunts; in another version, they were hardy forest folk who lived in dugouts, told tales in the dark and wove branches together to defend their territory. After their surrender they were locked up but soon escaped, returning to the woods to share a few last stories before they died.

Some people claimed they were raw recruits who starved one winter after eating grass and worms and cutting their flesh to drink blood. It was all part of a series of strange events during the big freeze that no one could explain. Rumour had it that they were actually British and involved in some sort of survival exercise. There was talk of suspended animation and genetic experiments. It's said that their names, scratched in bark, are there to this day – though no one, as yet, has found them. Their bodies were buried in unmarked graves.

In a few other versions they were ghost-soldiers who blew themselves up rather than be captured, or passed away quietly as the result of exposure. In these stories their camouflage was perfect and they became wood bark or brambles, blending in so no one could see them, or they patrolled at night as the wind in leaves. And in one account they were propaganda soldiers and never really there, and the so-called occupation was a ruse invented by counter-intelligence.

But people believed there were bodies in the woods. As a child I pictured myself moving tree to tree like a fugitive, shaking off my pursuers. I'd wriggle under fences and climb over walls to escape my confinement and run off to make my fortune, ending sleeping out where no one could discover me. I was wild yet fearful – asking myself what would happen if my parents didn't find me, but also imagining their reactions if they did. I was a boy in two worlds. In the bare front room, I was being questioned by my father dressed as a soldier. He was noting down my answers in a large black book. Beside him, my mother was staring at me and shaking her head. It seemed I was FOR IT.

In my other, outdoor world I was a Sioux Brave and the woods were my happy hunting grounds. Knowing the terrain, I could outwit anyone. I was in my element – backtracking often and wading downstream then climbing rocks and ducking into cover behind bushes.

The woods were much older than me. Their exact age was hard to guess but I knew they'd been there a lot longer than anyone in the family. They belonged to an original world where animals talked, children got lost and supernatural beings walked the forest floor. Things were *at large* in the woods – mainly unnamed mammals with their noses to the ground and shadowy figures lurking behind bushes. There were burn marks and dried blood on bark and stones. The mud in places was crisscrossed with giant footprints. The gangs who hung out there were rumoured to be hand in glove with criminals. They were known for their secret societies and savage initiation ceremonies.

Because the woods were out of bounds, they were an adventure. So I dreamed myself awake in them many times. Deep inside them were old water tanks that descended into darkness. They had what looked like shell holes in the top. When I climbed inside, I crouched on a ledge close to the water and waited. Being in there reminded me of times on the beach, buried in sand, when my thoughts went soft, dissolving into memories. It felt like a return to an original state of being.

He plays himself lost, pushing through the gap
between spring leaf and metal to the dog runs,
nettles and ivies over stone.

Out there are the semis, the veg lines and trellises
and paths behind sheds. There are fathers
fixing engines and women checking lists,
policemen, teachers and other children too,
with their nicknames, forcings and finger-pointing
smiles.

The wasteland gives him cover.

Inside he is shadowed, tunnelling towards greatness
on unexplored tracks; there are softwood watchers,
whispers, bodies close behind.

His mind's eye deepens to mud paths that lead
to overgrown water tanks pitted into earth.
Rust-dull and slow, with long stone drops, they
resonate drums.

His heart, perhaps?

And the night fears alone, groping down the path
to the newly-leafed corner where the gang leap out
to tie him to the fence.

The questions and mockery with leader smiling threats,
to the past-midnight dancers,
burn marks, bruises, stigmata and other-life dramas
of hospitals and tests.

Then footprints, detection,
following the great hunt, to the nightshade
and nettle patch and heel marks by the ditch.

Ending at the tanks, deep-breathed, resonant,
booming their great Os.

And the dreams there of descent
through half stops and flows to the deep-mind-cisterns,
with bowel shifts, squeezings and keyhole sweats
and near-sleep confinements singing in his head.

to echo back what?

When I returned from my dream I was in a strange place. The trees had closed in and the paths had petered out. Like a traveller in a story I'd lost my bearings and there was no turning back. It was cold and dark and the sun was going down.

Of course I knew what was happening. I'd stepped from one dream to another and my childhood fears had taken over. The woods were inside me. They were my feelings when I climbed the stairs and reached for the light switch. They were there all day waiting behind doors with a net to catch me, and they lurked in corners and cupboards, ready to jump out. Their shadow was everywhere, hidden behind curtains and at the mirror's edge, dodging out of sight when I turned to face them. Sometimes they were angry so I tried to placate them, calling them my friends and agreeing to what they said; at other times they asked trick questions or chanted single words; mostly they were just *there*, as breathers and pursuers with snail-like mouths flattened against glass. And it was their other-worldly calls I blocked out at night with my head beneath the pillow, telling myself no one was in the room. I was alone in the dark, surrounded by ghosts and wishing I wasn't there …

―― *Sue* ――

Leslie: As a visiting author, how do you work to stimulate the children's literary imagination?
Sue: Children are easy and rewarding, and give much more than adults. In primary school their imaginations are still a significant part of who they are, how they think and what they enjoy. So they're receptive and creative. I just offer them stimuli and outlets. I always use extracts from my own books to illustrate the fun of imagery, so that they can play with it too – or, with older students, to show how dark, mysterious or sad words can be. In secondary schools we look at psychology and feelings and I show them ways to access a character of their own. The aim is to inspire them to read by showing them how exciting stories are, and the impact and versatility of language. I always plan afresh and every time I'm booked as an author in school, someone astonishes me with a new response, an original idea, a memorable phrase. It's tiring but thrilling.

―― *Leslie* ――

Sometimes in the woods I see things. They appear as pop-ups at the limits of my vision. Everything about them is uncertain and liminal, so I don't know for sure whether they're out there or figures in my head. But I keep on seeing them. They make me think of childhood and borderline experiences – except now, in adulthood, I treat them lightly, taking in their shapes and keeping my distance. Sometimes I'm reminded of Rimbaud's *deliberate derangement of the senses* – but without the wildness, just for interest. At other times I try to catch them out, pretending not to notice, then turning sharply or stopping unexpectedly. It's as if I'm playing *What's the time Mr Wolf?* to wrong-foot my own mind. It's what Dali called his paranoiac-critical method: making a branch into a frame, a sunlit patch into a Dantesque cave, a crossing path into the beginning of a story ...

But walking with Sue in the woods was different. Being together made it safe. We were moving slowly, taking in everything and making it last. Like children in a fairground we were living the experience.

And the story?

That was in our heads, made up, invented, adapted, imagined ...

Looking back, I don't wood-walk anymore. My legs won't go the distance. But the memories remain strong. Stronger, perhaps, for being imagined. So I'm rambling through trees with Sue and stopping to look out. We're travellers in a painting by Claude with oversized trees shading dark pools and mythological characters. And in that landscape we're being transported to places we've never seen. It's an imaginary, retrospective, elegiac exploration of what lies beyond.

And we're still walking.

REWRITING THE SELF

—— *Sue* ——

Leslie: Who are your favourite authors – why them?

Sue: Until I was about thirty-five I only read classics and would have answered, George Eliot, Jane Austen, Dickens, Tolstoy and Dostoevsky. George Eliot is for me quite matchless. I'm in awe of her profound, generous and intricate understanding of humanity, her intellect and devastatingly elegant, witty prose. I've become a great admirer of Carol Shields, Anne Tyler, Elizabeth Strout, Barbara Kingsolver and Marilynne Robinson, but my favourite living author is Susan Fletcher, author of *Corrag* and *Eve Green*. It's hard to explain a connection between a writer and reader but I feel it powerfully when I'm absorbed in her work. It's a kind of love, and I dare to suggest it's soul to soul. Like all great writing, hers transports totally and convinces utterly. Her characters are fully and intimately realised, and there's a beauty to her simple style which can be richly sensual. I don't think I can enjoy a novel, however clever the author or individual the voice, unless there's compassion at the heart of it. I avoid cold, clinical fiction that treats writing as an exercise or presents people as selfishly dysfunctional. A fine novel has spirit and the kind of truth it offers should support life, not undermine it.

—— *Leslie* ——

Signing as an author in a bookshop is a blindfold tail-on-the-donkey activity. You never know when it's going to come good. It's also a set-piece gesture, with a hidden element of bluff. *Keep smiling* is the rule, even when there's nothing much doing.

Signing has its own performance rules, similar to stand-up. So the first 20 seconds are vital, and having a script helps, but off-the-cuff remarks usually work best. Often, it's the personal connection that drives the sale. In any case if you stop to think or push too hard it'll probably come out all wrong. As in sport, practice is vital, but belief is everything.

Signings are about reading people but not assuming anything, and welcoming their interest, regardless …

Generally, signings bring out the best and worst in people. So you might have to offer flyers or hold up a book while people walk past exchanging remarks such as:

'Who's that?"

"I don't know."

"Never heard of him."

Other people might stop to tell you about *their* books or hard-luck stories. And there are always the sightseers who want to look and ask questions then pass on to the next experience … But a few people will enter the shop with an expression that says *I'm keen*. They may not buy, but real interest is a lot better than mild amusement or standoffish smiles.

Signing is the author's one special power. It's a shared promise, like the child's note with a map that leads to the treasure. And there's a DNA factor about that squiggle on paper. It's a way of saying *this book has a life of its own*.

But in practice signing is a retail transaction – better described as hanging around in shops hoping to flog books. The aim is to impress, look good, speak clearly, and smile for the camera.

Part of the problem is money. In a materialistic society people are encouraged to judge their encounters by *what's in it for me*. So it's all about costing their time or striking a deal, or at least defending themselves against being cheated.

So authors, when they're signing, face a number of problems. These include:

The belief that an unknown writer must be second-rate and is therefore best avoided.

A fear than authors, like beggars, want something.

The thought that to stop and talk might lead, out of guilt or sympathy, to buying a book.

An idea that authors are self-obsessed evangelists who lack all social skills and go on and on and on.

An aversion to authors who name-drop or tell long complicated stories about being cheated by the book world.

A belief that authors are *up to something*; so a signing is a con trick designed to glamorise unwanted goods.

Cynicism, like yawning, is catching. Selling books is a state of mind. And everyone believes they've a book in them.

So why do authors sign?

Is it out of necessity – to chat to people while putting the books *out there*? Or maybe it's the inner-author as observer and commentator who won't give up? Then again, could it be out of awkwardness, oddness, difference, to get our own back? Or maybe just because authors do ...?

—— *Sue* ——

Leslie: What do your stories have in common? Which ones stand out as different?

Sue: In my stories for children I explore fantasy, historical, futuristic, mystery, humour, sci-fi ... and contemporary, real-world fiction where everything must feel utterly believable. Much as I enjoy challenging myself with new genres – and that's particularly true of my *world of Doctor Who* book, *Avatars of the Intelligence*, which I was reluctantly persuaded to write – I'm most at home writing stories that, for adult or younger readers, reflect life as it's lived now. It's always about relationships and feelings – even in *I am me*, my picture book for People not Borders, which helps very young readers to understand the experience of a young refugee coming to the U.K. That stands out as different because I use rhyme – even though I'm usually averse to that, to the point of allergic reaction! I've tried to avoid all distortion, shunned the obvious and aimed for freshness and integrity.

My adult short story collections are exceptions too, in that I had to find out what can be done in a few thousand words by reading and rereading the best, and find various approaches in order to fulfil my goal of diversity. I loved this way of writing so much that after thirty short stories I had to tell myself to take a break!

I could have answered that my YA Tudor novel, *Hue and Cry*, is the only one in which characters are murdered – not because I planned any kind of violence, which I avoid as a reader and writer, but because it became inevitable. Once a book begins, it takes shape, and developments consistent with the characters and context can't be resisted.

What unites all my books? Characters who, being individual, don't or won't fit in, resist in some way, or are experiencing emotional difficulties. A belief in love and its power to effect change and outlive death – I kept killing off parents for a while after my father died – and, almost always and sometimes overtly, my passionate commitment to social and environmental justice. As Michael Morpurgo wrote to me recently, "Perhaps only stories can change things."

―― Cy ――

I've had a lot of good times associated with cigarettes. In childhood my sister and I would pass through a magical curtain of cigarette smoke, moving from the sunlit gardens where we played at Narnia to the dim interior of the Farnham Maltings with our parents dancing to The Real Ale and Thunder Band. And on Christmas morning thick curls, like the ghost of Father Christmas's beard, hung in an atmosphere charged with cigarette fumes and alcohol.

But from the images of film noir detectives to the writings of Dennis Potter, I was born and raised with smoking. In my mind the *Evil Nick O'Teen*, invented in an early 80's anti-smoking campaign, was a far more attractive character than his opposite number, the goody-two-shoes Superman, clean-cut and wholesome. To me the ideal was the Rolling Stones photographed inside the cover of *High Tide and Green Grass* with an ever-present cigarette hanging from their lips.

It was through sharing a cigarette during a long hot day's filming with Director of Photography Al Ronald, that *The Electric Head* was born. Al was a talented young, long-haired Glaswegian in a black leather Stetson who, like me, had stepped out in need of a smoke. I was happy to oblige and soon not only were we sharing cigarettes but a surreal sense of humour and a long list of influences and obsessions. From B movie horror we moved through Spike Milligan and Douglas Adams to re-enacting our favourite League of Gentlemen and Python sketches, laying the groundwork for what was to become our double act.

—— Leslie ——

The surprise was so great that when they told me on the telephone I didn't know what to say. I'd worked out a speech about the years it had taken and being so long in the wilderness that I'd given up hope. I'd joke about the loo-roll novels, the cushions stuffed with rejection slips and the hallway blocked with self-addressed envelopes. Half the money was going to a charity, one that provided support for neglected authors (and money for their funerals), the other half to a foundation for promising writers – old ones, ugly ones, and those who filled their shelves with unsold copies of their latest book then burned them to keep warm.

When the time came to write a piece about how it felt to win I'd sidestep promo, bin those clichés about being grateful/humbled/honoured, and tell it as it is – a lottery, based on fashion, all cranked up for the benefit of sales. In the magazine interviews I'd confess to rereading my novel at night, uncritically, obsessively, and writing fan mail to myself. I'd talk about my name on the cover of a set book, a classic, force-fed to children and hated by teachers, or receiving a medal for services to literature as I joined the list of *greats*. I'd gloat over seeing my book in the hands of film stars, featured in quiz shows, or bulging from the pockets of men working on high buildings. And when it came to the ceremony I'd either set my critics forfeits – 1,000 lines copied from my novel – or I'd send in my representative who'd accept the cheque, wave like royalty and leave saying nothing.

I'd celebrate, of course. My name would be everywhere. And soon there'd be a film. In the months that followed I'd employ assistants who'd sit at my feet, write to my dictation and churn out *concept books* that I'd touch up then sign off as finished. I'd become a movement, a school of thought, with a published manifesto and weekend conferences and courses taught in select universities. There'd be streets named after me, a day on the calendar, and a yearly festival with flags and badges and stickers and T-shirts printed with quotes from my writings.

Then without warning, as if I was a character from my own prize-winning novel, my fortunes changed. At first it seemed like a temporary dip, with two-star reviews and a slowdown in sales, but then it spiralled with lawsuits and talk of plagiarism and critical exposés, leading to rows in public, readers taking sides and boycotts of my readings.

In the story arc that followed I lost heart, took to drink, had arguments with myself, then gave up writing and dropped to the bottom.

Years later I'm alone in my flat, writing again, with cushions stuffed with rejection slips and the hallway blocked with returned SAEs ...

I'm still waiting for that phone call.

—— *Cy* ——

I picture Al Ronald and myself as an explosion of colour. There was an immense joy and a freedom in *The Head*. Together we lived in a bizarre world, playing numerous crazy characters who belonged on both sides of the smoker's curtain.

Scripting *The Electric Head* was often a random process, like the cut-ups of Burroughs or the sound poems of Dadaists. Deliberately so. When we wrote material in our *Electric Shed* we took risks, throwing words and ideas in the air. It was the resulting unlikely word combinations that often made us laugh. For instance, *The Nicole Kidman Fingermouse Head Transplant Clinic*, or *Maple Pecan Biscuit Cake* – a phrase we'd spotted on a menu in the Naked Man Café in Settle, Lancashire, as we relaxed after filming a sequence in the snow.

Another example of throwing together a mishmash of surreal expressions was *The Lunch Doctor* sketch – a satire on a TV blind-date food show. Our version veered from a love triangle involving a ballet dancer named Joseph Stalin to buying freeze-dried GM children on the Internet. One of my favourite moments occurred while performing in a tiny attic-theatre above a pub. In the middle of our *St Peter and The Viking* Sketch, with me sporting angel wings and Al wearing a furry Viking cape and helmet, some drunken lads looking for the toilet knocked on the door, giving me the opportunity to say, "It sounds like someone's knocking on heaven's door." The sketch asked big questions about theology and organised religion (including "How can one enjoy heaven if one's atheist friends and family are burning in the pit of hell for eternity?"). It came out of a process of Al and me tossing ideas at each other mercilessly.

Our costumes, too, were like the characters one might see lurking in a surrealist painting and the gadgets were what one might discover in the wings of a Bonzo gig:

A pygmy hippo head mask

A man in a jar.

A *taxidised* aubergine with false eyes.

A children's electronic plastic guitar.

Two fish-shaped swords sculpted out of air-drying clay and painted one green, one red (in homage to Sith and Jedi lightsabres).

Some flashing conch-shell earphones.
The Telepathy Helmet.
My pride and joy, The Telepathy Helmet, was a labour of love. Its base was a silver-sprayed builder's hard-hat with attached flashing LED lights removed from my son's toys (with permission – he now tells me he always thought he might be able to own the helmet afterwards) along with electronic parts that bleeped or played tunes and a silver-sprayed *eagle-eyes* Action Man head we found down the back of an old sofa. I remember my mother-in-law discovering me cross-legged on the kitchen floor constructing it. She looked worried. Was this the type of activity a sensible grown-up husband and father should really be engaged in?

—— *Leslie* ——

My imaginary biography seemed like a good idea. Written by a friend as a limited edition and tagged as literary, the book set out to surprise, taking its readers into unfamiliar territory. I shared its growing pains and my friend's high hopes as it matured and developed. Now that friend, who prefers to stay anonymous, has cut off all ties with book and publisher and is threatening to sue.

Let me explain why.

The first draft was rejected as *action-lite*, the second as *academic* and the third as *overwritten*. The hard edit that followed was a lesson in unarmed combat. In the end, you could say we rolled over. The book's style now hits you where it hurts. Badged as minimalist, it's fast, it's takeaway, it doesn't outstay its welcome. It's aimed at TV.

The editor who first worked on it was a market wonk, a top influencer who invented his own brand. He called it "Geeks Gossip – a cross between Dirty Realism and #trendingaction." Later, when he left the publisher, a designer took over. She wanted flair, good lines and awareness, and a place at the table. It needed *the look, the perfect finish* to entice the reader in. "Think of it as a dinner party," she said. "Make it tasteful, season and garnish it, but keep it measured, and add in jokes to keep it going."

When she too left the publisher, a surgeon took over. His style was invasive. He talked about Occam's razor – a bare-bones job cutting out adjectives, chopping adverbs and ditching flashback, with no passive tense. After all, he said, who wants to pick through ploddy asides or yawn-making detail? "Avanti!" he cried as he blue-penned description, killing off characters, ramping-up conflict and adding in darkness. What began as a memoir turned into a thriller with an underworld journey, damage, dysfunction and a corrosive ending.

The next editor wanted to reach a younger audience. For her it needed a film-type car chase, a mission with gadgets, and a celebrity lock-up where all the characters got hurt or tortured. The genre was important, too, connecting with women through paranormal romance and men through action-adventure. She also required quick shifts in scene, a brainteasing plotline, intertextual games and unattributed dialogue.

After that the text was pitched for acceptance through Finance and Marketing, emerging slimmed down, re-badged and edited by lawyers.

When it hit the streets it was hailed as *authentic*, a masterly, first-time, straight-from-the-shoulder tour de force.

When the interviews began and my true story emerged, the book was given a makeover and reclassified as fiction. After a title change it disappeared, then came back for a while as a second-hand oddity, a collector's item. More recently, it's been listed in online libraries as out of print, possibly imaginary, minus a cover, with authorship doubtful. In one listing it's treated as a hoax, a faked-up MS invented as a happening.

So where's my book today?

In my dreams when I read it, the pages are blank.

"Not everyone's got a book in them," I hear a voice say.

I think of it as a lost voice, a shadow over water, a message in a bottle.

Sometimes, in the night, I search for it out of the window like a strange constellation or a Victorian folly.

The biographer friend, of course is me. It wasn't ever published.

——— *Sue* ———

Leslie: How does your imagination work?

Sue: For a soft, shy and sensitive person I have a pretty tough imagination. I'm conscious as a reader that it doesn't always let me go when I put down the book, and that's disorientating. It can take a while, if I'm emotionally involved as a writer too, to find my way back into the reality of my own world. The experiences I've imagined for my characters can leave me unreachable even to myself. My imagination has a lot more stamina than I do, and I'm not happy when it's shut down! So through a two sentence conversation at the breakfast table about a friend's health just now, I pictured him in a surgery (as well as in an armchair by a window last time we saw him), imagined his thin, bare arm and a needle, saw another story board image of him and his wife at a zoo with a child and foresaw a scene from the future in which his wife sits between us in the cab of a lorry and tells us about his health. Of course we're all imaginative beings but I have a feeling my imagination doesn't let up often and when it has to, because I'm tired and at a dry, business-type meeting, I'm disturbed and disaffected. If imagination won't serve, I'm helpless and panicky.

The storytelling reflex is sometimes inappropriate and unhelpful, though. When coming home and reporting on an encounter with a friend, I don't tend to deliver the one sentence headline, but the long narrative with character details. Asked for help interpreting the satnav in the car, I sometimes begin something of a story when there's no time to follow one! I'm an instinctive person rather than a logical thinker. This makes me fast – as a writer, taking action I believe in, shopping and cooking. But I struggle and become slow to learn with technology, maps and instructions. I retain stories better than facts, and while my memory has limited capacity for information that isn't personal, its storage space for details people have shared with me is extensive! When I'm listening to a friend my imagination is very active. Yes, I make connections and will offer my own experiential echoes or contrasts, but mostly I'm there, in their lives, imagining what it's like to be them. I love people and their unique, complex, interior stories. Nothing interests me more.

—— Cy ——

When filming, Al Ronald and I improvised, sometimes wildly. From Al's naked back garden snow-burials, to us in motorcycle gear on children's scooters plunging into the Thames in January, we kept pushing ourselves to the limit. But behind our creative mayhem lay Al's painstaking work stripping down and rewriting our material. He edited and directed a rambling script I'd written called *The Secret Diary of a Jobseeker* into the basis of *The Cracks Are Showing*, with us throwing ideas back and forth via email overseen by Ali MacPhail until it became a tight, satirical comedy pilot for Babycow with me as Mr Scrote, Al's nemesis, who embodied everything that's wrong with bureaucracy and conservative, Christian extremism.

The material for our scripts often grew out of personal life experiences, some of them obsessional. One source was my boyhood adventure world with action figures free-climbing bookshelves crammed with HG Wells and Jules Verne. As a boy I often pictured myself as Doug McClure in the Ray Harryhausen films, or Sinbad the Sailor from *The Arabian Nights*. Coming from an old naval family, I grew up looking out across the waves at the distant horizon. At bedtime as a boy I would imagine I was David Attenborough squeezing through an underground passageway with my torch. In my early teens my passion for real or fantastical travel led me to Michael Palin's *Around the World in Eighty Days* and then *Lila* by Robert M Pirsig.

Many years later I watched *Long Way Round* with my Dad on our last Christmas, when he was dying of cancer. We both enjoyed it, because we both dreamed of riding off on quests ourselves, sharing a love of Pirsig's and Che Guevara's books on the subject. I later made a spoof version of it with Al, mixing in ideas from *Gulliver's Travels*, because the juxtaposition of the two, with a lot of silliness thrown in, promised to be hilarious. I also hoped Dad would have enjoyed the joke.

My dad's world of jazz, whisky and cigarette smoke is still very much part of who I am. As a boy, the blue/green stripes and gold lettering of his ever-present packet of Players No. 6 were imprinted on my retina as a symbol of what it meant to be cool. With a carved African ashtray beside him and a bottle of Glenfiddich close at hand, he'd listen, cross-legged on our Persian rug, to Miles Davis and Roland Kirk with a blue cloud hanging above his curly black hair. Just as the rug's pattern showed the rivers  of the paradise garden, so the rivers of jazz, smoke, whisky and conversation flowed in and out of him. Looking back I see him, shaped like a giant Buddha in the middle of that garden, together with me, the tiny figure of a boy, staring up at him.

―― *Leslie* ――

Dear Agent,
My name is État Éilsel. I'm submitting my novel EVIL OLIVE. My father, who's a TV entertainer and knows your CEO, suggested I tried you. I've included the first three chapters, a CV and a synopsis.
I hope to hear from you soon.

Dear Agent,
You ask about promotion.
My product-book has plenty of hooks for readers. Lots of blood. A peephole scene with hot bodies. Battle set-pieces with mind-swords and disappearance-suits. Alpha males, pets, zombies, avatars and exotic locations.
As mentioned in my CV, I'm a Karaoke-novelist. In my video-promos I'm a postmodern D'Arcy, a tongue-in cheek James Bond and a Magic Realist Peter Pan. When I'm Dracula I sink my teeth into my own books and declare them super-tasty.
Yum yum.
I hope that answers your question.

Dear Agent,
Thanks for your new questions.
One of my platforms is food for readers. I make up surprise mixtures and serve them at signings. Cheese with chocolate, peppered toast, tomato brownies with chilli custard and my personal fav – muesli with wine.
Another platform is bookshop parties. Wearing a clown hat with bells on, I hand out balloons, bags of sweets, cardboard hats and plastic roses. If there are requests, I'll sing and dance and strip to my undies to sell a book.
My target audience are people who want to read about themselves – and let's face it, that's all of us.
And my unique selling point? My novel's title is a palindrome.

BTW, what do you think about the first three chapters of my book?

Dear Agent,

You ask if I've any more promo ideas.

I see myself as an author-showman. My novels are events. At signings, I wear a Superman costume and balance on book piles while holding a pen between my teeth. I tear copies of my novels in half with my bare hands then hide them around the bookshop. The first person to put together a complete set gets a priority pass to my next signing.

Online I run prize draws with rewards for loyalty and guess-the-character quizzes with cut-up quotes from my books. I've boxes and boxes of T-shirts and bookmarks and badges and armbands ready to give away.

Now a question from me: do you want the rest of my book?

Dear Agent,

You mention personality. I'm one. I have *je ne sais quoi*, IT, charisma; I'm hot, top of the list, Marmite.

This begins to feel like the X Factor.

What about my book?

Dear Agent,

I haven't heard from you for months. You're out to lunch or on holiday, permanent. Thanks for nothing.

How about if I join the Foreign Legion, and write about it?

―― *Sue* ――

Leslie: How has your imaginative life changed?
Sue: Looking back to write for this book, I became the child I used to be. I didn't expect that and of course it wasn't total, or magic, but I relived the feelings. Not so much the scenes recreated, some of which are imaginary but emotionally true, but what it was like to be the sensitive girl who loved stories, wanted to please and was afraid of all kinds of things besides rats and dogs, but also deeply happy to be loved. Many people who know me now, as a confident speaker for one of the causes I embrace, or as a visiting author in school, will find it hard to square that child with the woman I am in my early sixties. Although I'm making progress with dogs, I still live with all kinds of fears, some of them silly. When I first went up to the fracking protest at Preston New Road, I was anxious about the connections, getting the right bus in Preston and getting back in time for the train home. That was before I was asked to speak! But fear is a form of imagination, a recognition of the plethora of possibilities that make stories interesting. The important part, as I discovered eventually with my alopecia, is to resist the fear, and do and be what you must – to be true to who you are. We are all capable of courage and adventure and perhaps stories help with that, because isn't it the definition of a fictional hero? Part of my challenge as a writer is to imagine ways my characters can resist, overcome, find the courage to be themselves, defend a friend, defeat the force of darkness even if it's everyday prejudice rather than an evil baddie like Moro in my book *The Dreamer*. Imagination is also a prerequisite for empathy, and that's what makes stories so important for our humanity. You could say that by helping us to understand, they teach us to love.

―― *Leslie* ――

Sometimes Will thought of himself as the perfect phrase-maker. In his head he called himself *Will the Word-King*. But when asked what he meant by something he'd said, he usually smiled and went silent. For him, choosing words was an act of faith, and in any case he didn't want to let other people into his secrets. Because if they got inside his mind they might think him crazy. Of course they couldn't ever know him, not really, Will made certain of that. The world he lived in was a thought-bubble-space where he talked to himself and answered his own questions – keeping them quiet when he could. But of course, awake or asleep, the words were always there. They were his stops and starts, his voices heard in passing – soon forgotten when he got home – crazy phrases in a book or scribbled on paper, late-night rhythms running through his head … They went on … they went on …

Will's sister, Joan, ran. In her dreams she had wings on her feet and flew cross-country. When she ran downhill her legs took over. On the flat with the wind behind her, she was all skin and bone with muscles, pumping. When she ran the back straight she was in the zone, and when she sprinted for the line the earth moved, not her.

At the end of her run, Joan imagined herself jumping a hedge to land in her own front garden. After supper, she saw herself on TV as a fly zigzagging on the screen. When she woke next morning she set off again, best foot forward. Her legs had rhythm. Like breathing, they took their orders from the autonomic system.

Will and Joan met in a children's book. They were the pair who climbed the hill, who out-sang the birds, who named everything they saw, who called out to each other as they slipped and fell …

When Will got to the bottom he'd grown up. Holding his head, he rocked back and forth. Inside was a chaos of voices.

Joan told him to jump up and write. She'd learned that through running. If you lost your footing you got straight back up. "Don't stop," she said. "Just keep writing. Words can't stop you."

Will wrote his name. He wrote it once on the back of his hand, another time on a wall, again in history, then over and over on paper and in all the hidden places. And the world took notice, but forgot Joan.

The consequences were they became part of each other's back story.

The moral is that one person leads to another.

―― *Sue* ――

The courtroom tilted under her feet so the judge loomed over her, in a kind of balcony where no one ever asked the whereabouts of a lovesick teen. His wig looked thatched and powdered and his mouth widened large around a tongue she feared might drip. His teeth might have been as old as the law. At his right hand and his left, to take no chances, were attendants in robes with red cushions on which they balanced champagne flutes, caviar, olives and cigars.

She felt like a child who had strolled unwittingly into the wrong kind of book where children were eaten.

"The defendant is charged, my lord, with increasing and explicit activism ..."

"On the ground? Pesky protest?" the judge interrupted, reaching for the glass and drinking like water in a desert.

"Indeed, my lord, repeatedly, and often with a placard reading WHAT LOVE REQUIRES."

The attendants gasped. One attendant on an attendant was obliged to use a fan for cooling purposes and another needed sal volatile.

"But the prisoner's offences are not only on the ground."

"There's more?!" The judge needed more, in fact, and the champagne was quickly supplied and utilised.

"We are here to consider offences ON THE PAGE."

The shock around her was palpable. Should she feel ashamed? What followed, as she stood silent and exposed, was a stream of evidence in the shape of books slammed down like fists on olde wooden surfaces and offered to the judge for examination with rubber gloves.

"And some of these, my lord, are for CHILDREN!"

"I'm shocked," slurred the judge, pushing away the paperback copies of *The Waterhouse Girl, Crazy Daise, Shutdown* and *Start* as if they might contaminate.

"And this so-called FANTASY," continued the attorney for the prosecution, brandishing *The Dreamer,* is clearly meant to discredit fracking!"

"FRACK-ING! FRACK-ING!" chorused the attendants, punching the air.

The judge glared down, his body stretching and creaking as it towered higher, but his head lowered closer to her own like Nessie to a boat.

"Indeedy. A wonderful business opportunity compromised by yurt-dwellers who dance naked at full moon and drink kale."

"But there's more ... and here, my lord, I am obliged to offer you a device."

"My snuff cascader?" cried the judge, hopefully. "I left it in the billiards room."

The prosecutor sent a minion on that mission but handed the judge a laptop with the warning that the on-screen content might offend.

"A pay-as-you-feel e-book about WOMEN who use their fame to make exhibitions of themselves about CLIMATE CHANGE!"

The yawn that erupted was passed from mouth to mouth around the courtroom like a wave in a stadium.

"And, lastly, my lord, *For Life* ..."

"Oh definitely. At least! Send her down. Case closed." The judge's hammer was raised to fall but the prosecutor used a step ladder to whisper in his ear.

"All right, all right. If we must. Lunch won't wait," muttered the judge, waving a hand.

"Posted online every week, my lord, about rebelling. Outwardly a fiction with characters. About taking over Waterloo Bridge – where the accused misspent six days – to try to force government action."

Laughter swelled. The woman heard the last word echoed like a punchline.

"Climate action?" yelled the judge. "What action?"

The woman opened her mouth to suggest some but PING!! She found a plastic hand on the end of a large spring clamped to her mouth.

"Are you trying to tell me," the judge began, "that this miscreant believes in STORIES? Silly old make-believe stories?" He shrivelled his eyes at the woman in the dock. "Do you?"

"I do," said the woman. "They can change the world."

The silence was stunning. Was it fear?

"I've heard enough," spat the judge. The woman wiped her scalp. "You are charged with a particularly unsavoury kind of activism in fiction and faction and stories and all that airy-fairy, arty-farty terrorist nonsense." He gulped more champagne, some of which dribbled from glass to chin. "How do you plead?"

The woman's smile wasn't big or bright. It came from a jagged place where wings tore.

"Guilty," she said.

Leslie

My survival kit as an author:

Telling myself that writing's a long silence, like solo walking.
Believing my book's well-written while regretting every word.
Not counting the cost, or dreaming of fame.
Imagining myself planting seeds, naming flowers, deadheading.
Seeing writing as meditation.
Allowing the words to fly, run free, have their way.
Drilling out flaws, hacking out sections, filling holes.
Staying in the moment.
Whistling in the dark.
Interrogating text.
Using dictionaries, fact-finders, Wiki, Thesaurus.
Thinking of Mrs Dalloway, the Odyssey, Alice.
Arranging holiday snaps in a brown and white album.
Finding surprises; digging up myths; collecting stones on a beach.
Spider climbing walls to look down from the ceiling on the child inside.
Picking locks, unscrewing fixtures, breaking seals, stripping wallpaper, rewiring circuits.
Lighting imaginary fires in the paradise garden.
Teasing out stories from the pictures in my head.
Blowing up balloons, taking the pulse, growing wings.
Retouching life.
Walking the labyrinth.
Dissecting dreams.
Developing a voice.
New worlds and feelings, old worlds put together, wheels within wheels.
Just writing.

IN THE LIBRARY OF THE MIND

—— *Leslie* ——

What Love Requires of Us

My trip to Shepherd's Bush Library might have been taken from the pages of a magic realist novel. It was urban and dream-like, featuring a stranger arriving in rush hour at a shopping centre that could have been a film set. Of course there was a back story: an author visit arranged by email, and advertised as a talk about *The Dream of Great Writing*. But the subtext given – thoughts drawn from my experience of books – was unlikely to appeal to my potential audience. After all, who would want to listen to an unknown 69 year-old author with a small-press background? And why on earth would that author continue, year on year, turning up at hard-to-find spots and addressing tiny audiences, most of them failed or wannabe authors, in order to sell a handful of books?

My answer was, and still is, provisional. It touches on childhood, on impossible dreams and hubristic fantasies and poetry in the head. There is in me an ideal world, a garden of all delights where I walk untouched, sharing my thoughts with the birds. I'm still that boy who ran for his life on the beach and ventured down overgrown farm tracks hoping to find words for elevated longings and promptings from below. It wasn't that I actually saw God, but I was hopeful – and afraid – so I held my breath and took my time. If there were angels I was only going to meet them if I believed, or acted as though I believed. So, like a faithful follower, I fixed my gaze on the sky and waited for the break when my words would come into their own and be heard and recognised.

But arriving at Shepherd's Bush was more like auditioning for a walk-on part in a B movie. The square had an unreal, abstract, CGI quality, as if it was a mock-up. It was modern, noir, and packed with commuters. I'd thought, from looking at the map, I'd be close to the library, but all I could see were illuminated signs and strangely-shaped buildings. What made it even stranger were the puzzled faces of the people I asked for directions, who all said they hadn't heard of the library.

My talk was due in forty minutes and the suitcase I was wheeling was a dead weight. I'd stuffed it chock-full of books. Bringing so many was absurd, of course, because although this kind of event was all about exposure – meaning questions about future novels, and zero sales – I needed my dream. After all I might strike lucky and meet someone big in the trade and suddenly, in a flash, everything would change. Or I might just say the open sesame word, and people would flock through the door, eager to hear my story. On a deeper level I'd become accustomed to my outsider status. It kept me free of all criticism, in a category of one. Because being unknown allowed me to admire my own resilience and see myself as ahead of my times – which explained my repeated failures with agents and writing competitions. I'd my own distinct voice; I believed I could write; so the fault was not in my stars but with *them*.

I was beginning to wonder if the library didn't exist, or the map I'd studied was out of date, but magic thinking kept me going. Maybe I'd get lucky and find a sign or I'd turn a corner and the library would be there – or maybe if I visualised and followed the images that came up, then that would do the trick. After all, I'd given talks about the imagination and quoted Einstein about its primacy over knowledge. In *My Imaginary Autobiography* blog I'd written about memory as a retrospective elaboration of an imagined past. In other pieces I'd talked about the power of language to re-imagine the self, changing speculation into fact – and in some of my poems I'd described that as a form of myth-making, bringing with it the danger of inflationary thinking.

So inside myself, I was living my experience as a Quixotic adventure carried out solo, against the odds. It was my own absurd, defiant bid for recognition, a private journey into nowhere; it was my Narrow Road to the Deep North, Journey to the Centre of the Earth and *Une Saison en Enfer* rolled into one, and my task was to memorise every detail with the aim of reworking it as a story ...

1.

I remember sneaking out of the house at night. It was my first youthful test of character, or that's how I saw it. At 14, I'd a key and I wanted to be out in the world on my own. Choosing a clear, cold night, I slipped down the village main street. It was the small hours and the houses were dark and silent and the pavements were empty. I was telling myself to step quietly like a spy. When a taxi passed by I hung back in the shadows, watching for faces peering around curtains. In the silence afterwards I could hear my own breathing. I felt my exposure, and my body was shaking as if I was on the run.

Hearing the words *pull yourself together* in my head, I tucked my hands into my pockets and walked on. The street sloped down to the harbour and a bare green space with a flagpole in the middle. On one side I could see the quay lit by a single streetlight, on the other, a row of cottages leading towards darkness. Feeling the wind against my face, I set out across grass. As I approached the flagpole I heard something rattling. It made me think of loose stones in a box. Forcing myself to look, I saw a thin metal wire slapping against wood. It was twitching like a muscle.

Leaving the green I walked to the end of the village. Ahead was darkness, and the sound of breaking waves. I'd been here before, but not usually alone and never at night. In my mind I saw myself as a kind of mental traveller, a poet-explorer about to face something wild and dangerous. As I passed the last house my legs stiffened, but fear kept me moving. Whatever was happening, it was too late to turn back.

Entering the dark, I followed a sandy track to a drop. Here I found a low rock to sit on and stare out to sea. The moon was up and the beach was visible as a shadowy strip. As my eyes adjusted I saw the waves running in, silver-white and streaky; in my mind, they were alive. I watched them break and spread their thin grey membranes across sand. As I watched, I imagined myself a castaway, searching for rescue. I'd been here so long I was in danger of forgetting where I'd come from, or even my own name. I pictured the low rock as my gravestone, inscribed with words about how often I'd sat here. Looking back from a made-up future, I could see it all. I'd a camera inside me, recording every detail, and my last dying wish was to preserve this moment as something special, a dream of my own, and make this wild, poetic place a part of me.

There'd been other times I'd been outdoors at night without my parents knowing. I'd crept out in winter in absolute secrecy, taking the alleyway at the end of our estate. Reaching the road I'd crossed to the locked park and squeezed through a hole in the fence. Inside was shadowy and overgrown, but I knew my way around. I followed the path by the bushes, treading carefully on gravel. I passed by the lawn and the frosted borders to arrive at the pavilion – a long low hut backing onto a football pitch. Checking no one could see me, I ducked behind the building and into the shadow of a large tree. My chest was tight and legs were unsteady. I knew what I'd come for, and the cold air made me both hot and breathless. Hearing an approaching car, I froze. What if my parents realised I'd gone? Worse still, if I was caught here … As the car came closer, I imagined police sirens followed by shouts and radio voices, then flashlights and dogs. The headlights closed in, illuminating the fence and the gate. For a second I thought the vehicle was going to turn in and my thoughts went dark, then the car swished by, continuing to the village. In the silence that followed, my mind came back; no one was after me. I was alone, unobserved, and ready to act.

I stayed for an hour by the bay, listening to the rhythm of the waves. A phrase came up, comparing the moonlight on water to white-hot ingots. I repeated it out loud, gazing at the beach. My camera-mind returned, fixing the scene as a snapshot, so I could go back to it whenever I wanted to. I believed that if I focused properly, the shapes and sounds would become imprinted, certainly for a while, possibly forever. I could be there and not-there just when I pleased, watching from a place outside the frame *and* at the centre. And yet what I saw was nothing extraordinary. I was sitting on a rock overlooking a bay … it was night time and I shouldn't be out … that was all. If there was something more then I'd made it happen – deliberately, consciously.

On the way home the weather had changed. The air felt damp. The moon had disappeared and a fine haze was blowing in from the sea. Mist sprays hung about the streetlights. There was a cloud of stillness gathered around the village.

Feeling the darkness closing in I didn't look back. I'd been to the edge, had my experience and now I was returning, much the same. If I'd changed, it wasn't that immediate or obvious. When I reached the front door, I slipped in and stood in the darkened hallway. Outside and inside, the world felt cold. The task now was to adjust to being ordinary.

In the park I was dodging through shadows. I'd stowed my clothes in a dry corner and now my own bare body was driving me forward. I was running wild, enjoying the frisson of excitement. Of course I knew it was crazy but there was a freedom about it; I was hot and cold and all in a lather. I was in my element.

Arriving at the lawn, I paused before stepping out in full view. This was my moment of maximum danger. It just took one pair of eyes, someone gazing idly from an upstairs window, and I'd be for it. Of course I'd smile, say it wasn't me and insist I'd been asleep, but from then on I'd be under suspicion. Word would get around and I'd be pointed at and talked about. I'd be the one they avoided whose name would live on, scrawled on desks and on toilet walls, known to everyone as *the strip-kid* and *the weirdo in the park*.

My feet felt alive against the grass. My chest was a shield against the cold air. In my mind I could hear the title of a film: *Nudes in the Snow*. I remembered seeing the words in a newspaper advert and being shocked. Now, I told myself, I was living them – in action, in my own private show. My blood was up, I was there without cover and no one could stop me. This was who I was.

Afterwards I pulled on my clothes and retraced my steps, trying to keep a distance between myself and my thoughts. I'd given in again, I'd disgraced myself and no one would respect me. Words like *never* and *shouldn't* ran through my head. By the time I reached home I was promising myself to be helpful and speak nicely to make up for what I'd done. I'd gone too far and dirtied myself and now only God could save me. The voices in my head told me, as I stepped inside the house, that I'd failed my test. There'd be no more nights out in the park.

2.

In my search for Shepherd's Bush Library I was dragging my suitcase up a ramp and across a brightly-lit highway. I was following a crowd in the general direction I'd memorised from studying a map. The road was raised up and we crossed it in stages, pausing for shelter on islands. I had to steady the case as I walked, using both hands to grip the pull-out handle. My attention was focused on getting across, but inwardly I was looking out from somewhere else: a place in my mind where anything might happen. It was part of a memory where I walked into a bare, wide space with the sun and wind in my face and my feet sinking into sand. In my memory – or my dream – I'd a sense of being both present and absent as the boy who'd run to the sea's edge and the man looking back. I could see both ways: back to the houses and out to the horizon. There were ships and seagulls and flags, and a vanishing point.

Suddenly I was alone and there was cold air and spray around me. I'd ventured too far and now I was struggling to return with the waves getting higher and the tide coming in. The sea was everywhere, filling up the air with siren-like calls. I was surrounded by its white noise, and yet I could hear, echoing quietly and persistently from somewhere further out, the voices of my parents.

Ignoring their warnings, I crossed the road. I knew, of course, as I turned into an estate, that my fear of lateness was a throwback. The whole of my childhood had been governed by fixed routines. In our house we had to account for each minute: what we were doing, or intended to do, and where we were at any given moment. There were laid down hours for eating, sleeping and getting up in the morning – and a whole host of petty restrictions involving timings and schedules that had to be applied for and granted before they were allowed.

Stopping in a backstreet, I checked my watch then walked on to a square where I asked for directions. As a man pointed to the north, I realised that the library was a long way off and time was running out. The wind had got up and rain was in the air. Suddenly I had a lost-child feeling. I was the story-boy alone in a wood – or a picture of a wood – with the trees all watching. It was dark and their branches had become arms and their leaves were hands, pulling me in. Somewhere in the distance I could hear a baritone singing *Der Erlkönig*. I'd been here hours, or so it seemed, and although I knew it was a dream, I'd a feeling that I was living in the moment. In an odd way, the trees were *me*, alive and actual, as indeed was the whole picture.

Crossing the motorway by an underpass, I struck out northwards. In my mind I was on the beach with storm clouds ahead. I was straining now, dragging the suitcase up slopes and along busy walkways. I'd had various illnesses, my legs and arms ached, but I was back in childhood outrunning my pursuers, and part of me was amazed at my strength. At the same time I knew, or feared, there'd be a payback. But I was resolved: I'd come this far, I was a survivor-author, who wrote against the odds. Like Macbeth I was *stepped in so far* ... whatever the cost, there was no turning back.

3.

At the age of nine I knew all the secret and hidden places. Walking the street I'd a mind-map of the back routes and cut-throughs that would make me hard to track. There were places where I'd turn in quickly and hide behind walls, bamboozling my pursuers and leaving them lost and scratching their heads. In my dreams I was a super-being who could see way ahead, and part of that power was that no one knew I had it. I was in charge: one word from me and it was so.

My head was full of stories. Usually unfinished, they came and went like adult conversation. Talk, talk, talk, my teacher called it, telling off the boys. What would she do, I wondered, if she knew what I knew; could see what I was seeing? There were so many possibilities...

In daydream one, the classroom was afloat. I was on deck wearing a tricorn and pointing a telescope towards land. My hand was steady and my back was straight. Roger, my First Mate was by me, saluting. "Aye, aye, captain," he barked.

In the second daydream, Roger the Mate and I were circling above the school. Looking down we saw the teacher, who was flying us on strings. The strings were multi-coloured, like maypole ribbons and strong as dog leads. Up here we were having fun like fairground kids, waltzing to tremolo guitars. The music came whooshing up from below in a gale of sound: *Ghost Riders in the Sky*, played with a twang. We were chewing pink gum and flicking paper pellets at the clouds. When the music stopped we crashed to earth, like the R101.

In daydream three, we bounced and somersaulted on the moon. We were space gymnasts who could flip between worlds, dark to light, calling out "Wheeeeee!" as we climbed rock-strewn ridges and hot-bum-skidded through dust.

In daydream four, Roger was a mutineer I disciplined then pardoned. The discipline involved hopping then kneeling while singing high notes; the pardon came with ice cream and fizzy drinks.

In reality he was my friend, Roger, who played with me in the shed, a flat-faced boy with slicked-back hair and sticky-out ears who squealed when it rained, drumming on the roof.

I didn't like his squealing; it was loud and shaky and cut through the air like a whistle. When he ran out of breath I was relieved, but irritated that he'd gone on so long. I tried not to feel that way, but Roger was an actor, and he knew how to annoy me. Playing the fool was his modus operandi. He claimed all sorts of things. One day he was Mowgli and hunted with big cats in the garden, the next he drove in the Monaco Grand Prix, at night he worked on solving murders and listening-in to suspects on the phone – not to mention his descent from Churchill, his pictures of ghosts, and his millionaire uncle's plan to shoot him to the moon. I poo-pooed it all, but behind my denials, I understood. Crazy-crazy was good. It was why we were friends. Because if I was honest I'd had the same fantasies, but my way of expressing them was different. I kept them hidden, in a dream-tight box, sealed inside myself. And what I spoke about to others was a version, or diversion. So when the rain hit, beating a rhythm on the corrugated roof, I made up a story.

"It's the sea," I said, rolling my eyes.

"Whaaat?" replied Roger.

"The sea rising. A hundred-foot wave, smashing into the shed."

"Oh, no."

"It's a silly story. But it's real. Listen, and I'll tell."

"You will?"

"Uh huh. Now, you heard of Narwhals?"

"Um, yes."

"So what do you know about them?"
"Not much."
"You mean NOT-A-THING?"
"Suppose so."
"Cross your heart and hope to die?"
"No ... not that."
"Ah well ... Narwhals came before people. Before anything. They had no heads and tails, just blobs, and they wriggled about in ice. And then one day something hit the ice. It wasn't a bird thing and it wasn't a plane thing and it wasn't a star. It was a no-thing. Yes, a nothing ... And it spread out like hot rain. And the rain made the ice open like an egg. And in the cracks there were skin bits and fin bits and a bone thing left sticking out like an icicle. Then the Narwhal swam off, using the bone thing to feel its way. But when it came to land it saw something. What it saw was em-pti-ness. EM-PTI-NESS, except for four legs and a soft heart. That was all. But Narwhal still liked it. So Narwhal crawled onto land ... and crawled and crawled and crawled and then ..."
"Yes?"
"Turned into something."
"What?"
"Guess."
"A spider?"
"No."
"People, like you and me?"
"No."
"A unicorn?"
"Nope."
"What, then?"
"Narwhal turned into rain. A wave of rain, a hundred-foot high."
"Like that?" Roger pointed upwards.
"Crashing into ice."
"But what *was* Narwhal?"

"Ah well, that's another story ..."

In daydream five, Roger and I were out on the shed roof, in warpaint, stripped to the waist, riding Narwhals bareback through the rain.

4.

On the outside, Shepherd's Bush Library looked like a pound shop without the signs. I walked past it twice, believing the block to be either empty or closed for the night. There were lights inside, but they seemed rather dim, and the name on the double doors was hard to read. But when I stepped inside I could see it was a busy, open-plan library with shelves at different angles and a waist-high counter facing the door. Behind the counter two assistants were peering at screens and talking to customers. They worked in a world of self-contained busyness. When they realised who I was, the older one, who introduced herself as Eleanor, led me to a central space with a cushioned seat and a low table facing a triple line of chairs. Speaking quietly, she asked me if there was anything I wanted.

"That's fine. I'll just set out my books," I said. I was aware of her watching so I didn't check the time, but I knew my talk was due.

"We're sorry," she said suddenly, "but our events manager can't be here. She sent her apologies."

I remember my reaction. A silent *what?* rising in my throat, but covered by a lightly-worded question. On the surface I was friendly and surprised and busy with my books; inside I was annoyed. At the same time, I'd half-expected it. The events officer had been hard to pin down. Her emails, involving big ideas and lots of promises, were usually followed by silence. The ultra-sincerity of her promises reminded me of a teenager saying, *trust me*.

So why had I turned up? A number of answers, some obvious, some less so.

Firstly, I'd been booked and by being there on time I was in the clear. I'd avoided responsibility and proved my credentials.

Secondly, I'd set out on a journey and the effort, regardless of outcome, gave it a kind of absurdist dignity.

Thirdly, a small part of me hoped that this could be THE turning point, when I'd be the counter-culture figure whose time had come – and as I waited I rehearsed the slights and brush-offs and failures to respond, naming the publishers who'd rejected my novel and watching them squirm as I took them to task in my speech accepting first place in the Booker ...

5.

When I'm writing about childhood I see a boy, quite often on his own, playing in the garden, or sitting in a room with his family. He's different from me. He's an outline or a drawing and his presence, though real, has a slightly spooky quality. Part of how I see him is the result of photos, so he's the boy with the pudding basin haircut whose arms and legs are too thin, or he's the smooth-faced boy with the *meant* (and manic) expression. And his face and his family's, seen through the lens, are time-lapsed, preoccupied and strangely detached.

If I place him in a story, it's with children who don't fit. Awkward, toothy kids like Roger in the shed and my other play-friend, Gillian, who lived close by in a detached house with her flighty, loud-voiced MOTHER. They were the sort of family my parents didn't like, calling her an out-of-hand girl brought up by a weak-willed father and *that woman.*

Of course words are dangerous. My parents threw them around defiantly, daring anybody to contradict their views. For them, the world was *a shambles,* nothing made sense and people weren't to be trusted.

Roger's parents were, if anything, more reactive than mine. They were ha-ha-ha-ha types who specialised in jokes at their target's expense, using words as kick-me notices to pin on someone's back. In their stories that person *copped it* or *got it in the neck* – often Roger was the clownie-slapstick-kid who always got it wrong. For them, it was shoot first ask questions later – and their barbed remarks, because they were delivered with a take-it-or-leave-it smile, were hard to counter.

What both families thrived on was accusation. So Roger's made fun while mine closed ranks against Gillian and her lot. According to them, her voice was too loud, she couldn't sit still and she behaved like a boy – all of which made her untrustworthy.

"Oh, *her*," my dad said at the mention of her name.

"What's that girl been up to now?" my mum said, when she discovered I'd been with her.

In the Q & A that followed, I claimed that she'd scared us or bribed us with sweets; Gillian was the brains behind everything.

And the truth about Gillian?

She did have powers. When Gillian entered the shed, Roger and I stopped talking. We wanted to be friends and share things with her, but didn't know how. "What you saying?" she'd call out, closing the door and silently staring.

"Didn't say a thing," Roger answered, looking my way.

"What you been saying behind my back?" she demanded. Her voice sounded strained, like an old recording.

"Nothing."

"Nothing?"

"Not much."

"What then?"

"Some words."

Gillian stepped up close to Roger. "I don't like words," she hissed, speaking slowly. "Words aren't good." Then she sighed and began to pace back and forth. "Sit down," she said, pointing to two chairs.

We did as we were told.

"Legs together. Arms folded."

Again, we obeyed.

"Eyes closed."

When Roger moved, she placed one hand on his head, calling, "You're in my power."

When I coughed, she touched my jaw. "You can't talk."

Then, when she'd warned us to keep still, Gillian removed both hands and began to sing: "The farmer's in his den, the farmer's in his den, EE-I-AD-I-O, the farmer's in his den."

She went on singing until she reached the words, "We all pat the bone." Here, Gillian pressed down on our shoulders. "Now stay, slaves. Eyes closed and no talking. You'll hear from me when you can move."

I remember the wait that followed. It was like sitting blindfolded in a cinema, picturing scenes to fit the soundtrack. I could hear Gillian's footsteps, the door clicking shut, Roger breathing, then a long silence ... Outside the birds sang, radio voices came and went, a plane passed over. Keeping my eyes shut, I could hear – or thought I could hear – Gillian on the lawn. She was marching up and down beside the shed, taking peeks in through the window. I could picture her face, distorted behind glass. Whether she was there, or in my mind only – the fear of her held me. I was shut indoors unable to get out, the dream had taken over, and I'd die there with Roger ...

6.

In Shepherd's Bush Library things were quiet. After ten minutes I was imagining myself, when I arrived home, telling my wife about zero attendance. It had happened before. Sue and I had arrived at a Leicester library after a long drive and been directed to some chairs squeezed into a corner by a window. It had the feel of a backstage area in an abandoned film set. Looking out, it was just before sunset, the shops and pavements were empty and there were no lights in the cinema opposite. Inside, there were a few head-down readers, who might have been placed there as extras, and an assistant behind a desk.

We were feeling bleak. We'd been invited, brought books and prompt cards, talked through our act, and now no one wanted to know.

After waiting fifteen minutes I sat down by Sue. "Maybe it's best if we don't get anyone."

She gazed out of the window. "You mean so we can go home?"

I nodded. "But I wonder what we'd do if anyone *did* arrive?"

"I suppose we'd have to turn them away."

"What about if we performed?"

"Performed? Even for one person?"

"Why not?"

"I don't think so. We'd talk to them, of course, but we couldn't really *do* anything."

I stood up. "Let's try."

"Try what?"

"If we can't talk books," I said, offering my hand, "at least we can dance."

Sue rose to join me. "You mean that?"

I nodded. "Call it a rehearsal. We'll dedicate it to our absent fans."

Sue laughed. As she took my hand the bleakness lifted and we slow-danced in a circle, shutting out the world.

In the Library I'd started my talk. After fifteen minutes, two women had arrived apologising for lateness, followed by a third. The two, wearing white and looking vaguely churchy, sat at the back, the third slipped into a seat at the side, close to Eleanor the librarian. Directly in front of me there were two rows of empty chairs. I'd seen actors playing to very small audiences; now I knew how they felt. The room had expanded or I'd got smaller; there was a gap in the air, a distancing, like a camera pulling back.

I began by reading my book's first sentence, asking them for predictions. After waiting, I suggested a few clues. Eleanor named a genre and the woman at the side nodded. When the other two remained silent I reread the sentence, picking out key words and what they might lead to. When no one responded, I read on, stopping at the end of the chapter and inviting comments. The group made a few then asked me about being an author. This time my answers seemed to interest them, with the women at the back asking questions and Eleanor chipping in. Suddenly I realised that the group were more interested in the person behind the writing than the books. They wanted to know *me*.

I shared a few ideas: technical ones about writing – standard moves and tricks of the trade – and thoughts about resilience, psychology and surviving as an author. When asked, I talked about the book trade with its lists and brands and hyped-up claims, returning quickly to writing.

I wanted to tell them about looking for the library, describing my search as an act of foolishness – like my writing. I'd take them with me to cliff-top lookouts and in-the-head missions, then on through moments of exposure stripped off in the dark. Yes, I'd been crazy – but intensely alive and all-too human. And if they asked me why, I'd tell them this was my *real* journey: a private, psychological, deep-soul thriller.

Of course, I didn't. It was too hard to explain. In any case, the writer's job wasn't that straightforward. I was here as the author, while at the same time seeing myself as a character in my book. I was in the middle, part-fiction, part-real, in a push-pull situation. And I knew on my library journey, or in the scene with Roger, how things could, at any moment, change.

How? Quite simple. I'd take the story further …

In the revised version, Gillian, after pacing the garden, returned. As she entered, cool air blew into the shed.

"Eyes open," she called, "and stand."

We obeyed.

She inspected. "Remember, I don't like words. Words aren't good."

We nodded.

Suddenly Gillian called out, "We all pat the bone!" beating a rhythm on our shoulders.

"EE-I-AD-I-O," she continued, beating our arms and across our backs, as if she was frisking us.

"Tell my dad," Roger said, squirming.

Gillian stared. There was a chill in the air. "So?" she said, patting his head. "Who's *he* then?"

"He's Tarzan. Wrestles alligators."

Gillian laughed. "Prisoner," she cried, squeezing his neck, "don't lie!" When Roger began to struggle she pat-whacked him, calling out, "Be still!" When he started to blubber she whacked harder, and when he sank to the floor she hauled him up and shoved a fist in his face.

Then Roger began to squeal. It was a small, whiny, lost-animal squeal.

"No," said Gillian, shaking him.

Roger's squeals became yelps.

"Stop it," she called.

His yelps went up a note.

"Shut up!" she cried, reaching for his mouth.

"I'll stop him," I said quickly, grabbing her arm.

Gillian turned. For a second I could see her struggling with herself. "You ...?" she said, glaring.

"I can try ..." I said, letting go of her arm.

As I spoke, Roger's yelps got louder. I could hear he was on the way to his whistle-squeal. There was nothing I could do.

"No!" cried Gillian, cuffing Roger's head. It was a glancing blow, but enough to stop him. He sat down heavily, looking much older. His shoulders had hunched and he was snivelling quietly, with the odd heavy sob.

The shed had gone cold. There was a stillness in the air, the world had emptied out, and nothing any more was certain.

Gillian stood back. "Now go. But *tell* and you know what happens." The shed walls echoed her words.

When I opened the door, it was damp and I could see Roger, shivering. My chest was tight and I was short of breath. It was as if we were in an airlock, being sucked out. Looking upwards the sky was steely-grey and threatening.

As we stepped out, the rain began to fall.

—— *Cy* ——

My good friend Dan always said I should *get a doctor's note*; he was fairly sure I was mad, certainly madder than he was. When I lived with him for around six months, he witnessed the repetitive ceremonies and obsessive routines I went through in order to enter the *real world*. A kind of camouflage and preparation, putting on my *whitecoat* self to venture out and blend in.

Whitecoat had a long history. I remember appearing for interview at an office job in a suit and white shirt with shoes that I'd polished like my father. Having been in the navy and then the police force he would spend a lot of time sitting on the back doorstep with a cloth and a pot of black polish, and I recall the sound of the brush flicking backward and forward with machine-like military precision until his boots were like two black, magical spirit mirrors. I'd taken the tie I wore for the interview from a sack of assorted clothing at my previous job. It was like a talisman to me, a piece of the asylum. It was mustard yellow with purple and turquoise paisley swirls, and unfashionably wide. I assumed the tie had once belonged to a patient there in the Sixties and been left behind, but for me it was like a sliver of reality in an unreal world. It was a secret sign that I didn't belong.

At home with Uncle Dan I became *Straitjacket*, wearing clothes that included Jackson-Pollock *painting trousers*, converse sneakers with artworks on the toes and a T-shirt with the word FREAK emblazoned across it. *Straitjacket* me understood Oscar Wilde's advice to, "Be yourself; everyone else is already taken," but in public I wore clothes carefully chosen to keep a low profile. I wanted to look like someone running the asylum as opposed to an inmate.

I've given *Straitjacket* many names: Icarus, Longpin The Hingemaker, Captain Absinthe, Legion, The Red Hornet and Biff The Amazing Mahogany Boy. Another version of Straitjacket, invented by my second wife, is *Yc* (Cy backwards). As the polar opposite of the even-tempered, reserved character, Yc appears in two phases: 1) The hungry force of the freed prisoner, hedonistic, self-destructive perhaps, emotional certainly, passionate and anarchic. 2) The boundless force of creative energy. It's in the second phase that I produce my best work. I've also learnt that the more the Straitjacket in me is subdued the more violently anarchic it becomes.

So when, and why did the split occur?

When I worked as a clerk in an office, Whitecoat was known as *The Faxman*. Of course, he was really only a roughly stapled-together facsimile of an office worker himself. Outwardly conformist, when alone at his desk Straitjacket would peek out as he began to fax poetry and artwork to the other offices in defiance of the dull, grey *work-world* in which he found himself. Straitjacket or *Biff* worked extremely hard to tear apart the mask he wore on a daily basis, to chip away at the facade.

This was the first time I became fully aware of the two different aspects of my personality. After all, the increasingly unstructured world of my evenings and weekends, filled with intoxication, music and dancing was so entirely at odds with the strict order of the quiet filing clerk. There was something Kafkaesque in the daily metamorphosis from one to the other.

The Faxman was so efficient that, where once three people had handled the job, it was now only him, and he prided himself on the swift and exact nature of his work. He was machine-like, inhuman and infallible – while inwardly reflecting on his own strange split. Was it, he wondered, to do with the brain's two hemispheres, dark and light, sanity and madness, or was it, at an atomic level, the idea that every particle has a shadow particle? He knew that alcohol often unlocked the Straitjacket and saw, in Blake's words (discovered later), that the *Prolific*

(Straitjackets) and *Devourers* (Whitecoats) were natural enemies.

I did have a Blakean vision once, looking down into my *asylum* tie. As the purple paisley swirls began to wave like seaweed underwater, I saw my tie as a crack, a hole in the texture of time, a veil lifted. I longed to dive into it. I believe Jung and many others have been on similar journeys into their unconscious and I needed to be wholly devoured in order to achieve a state of imago. I think it was said that Zeus had split mankind into two halves and the two opposites needed to clash at this point in my journey. One had to slay the other so that I could be reborn.

I left the office and moved into my friend Mr Alan's flat, carrying a black bin bag and my heavy concrete Buddha through a crowd of suited commuters. I was struggling against the tide like some odd Clownfish (another name I have often used for Straitjacket). I had found a job in the Invisible Hinge Factory next door to the office from which I'd finally escaped. It was a wonderfully Straitjacket-friendly environment. Although the work was dull and repetitive there was no need to hide. Amongst the dirt and grime there were many colourful characters  like John, a schizophrenic Christian with a physics degree, and Tall-Paul, a dreadlocked proponent of Tai Chi, who had just returned from travelling. I learnt a lot from their fierce daily discussions. John told me about string theory, particle physics and the Bible, and Paul explained Taoism. Even there, I was still powerfully split. At times I arrived at work so drunk that Tom our boss would send me home. Mr Alan had a wardrobe filled with duty free gin and cigarettes and had said that I could help myself so long as I kept a log of what I'd consumed. I ended up drinking myself toward oblivion – Straitjacket had taken complete control and he certainly wasn't one for abstaining.

For the majority of my adult life I've let one or the other of the two sides lead. Even now in my day job I wear the same shirt and suit Faxman wore all those years ago, although I occasionally expose a toned-down version of Straitjacket's creative energy. In shifting from one to the other, I've repeatedly gone through a cycle of destruction and creation. Systematically, Straitjacket chips away at the perfectly ordered world Whitecoat creates until it falls apart. Then he delights in the destruction and his artistic freedom until Whitecoat has to emerge from the rubble and rebuild his life again.

It's only as I write that I realise Straitjacket is the true me, the artist and poet whose dreams free the mind and make anything possible. It was Straitjacket who played imaginary games with my son, travelling through the *Wood Between the Worlds* or to the *Giants' Garden*, accompanied by Captain Barnabus and a Liverpudlian Werewolf called George, and inevitably meeting *Bonesy*, a genius time-travelling Skeleton boy, on the way.

Straitjacket has helped me to invent *incredible journeys* with my autistic clients, such as our hot-air balloon excursion to the North Pole along with Hans Asperger, Clint Eastwood and a talking giraffe.

Straitjacket also has the capacity to completely transform into other characters, such as the psychopath *Bern* – though I admit that sometimes, playing him on stage, I wasn't always altogether sure what he would think or say next.

I was once sitting on the sofa at a get-together of my first wife's family, next to her grandmother.

"Are you doing anything later?" she asked.

"No, no, just a quiet night in," I replied.

She looked into my eyes for a long while without speaking.
"Your eyes belie you," she said.
She saw Straitjacket in there, twinkling.

—— *Leslie* ——

In the library of my mind there are lots of half-read books. I keep them on the shelves, taking them down occasionally to dip into their pages. They're the unfinished fragments that make up my past. A few lie open on chairs and tables, where I left them. Arranged chronologically, they read like this:

1. An imaginary childhood scene where I'm walking around a bay with my dad. The tide's out and the rocks stretch as far as I can see. The wind blows about our faces; its odours keep me braced up. Being with my dad is a journey into unknown territory. I'm hearing his words, things he might have said, still present in my head. He's my last stand hero: a big, weatherworn man striding forward who knows where he's going. As we walk, although I'm right by him, he doesn't really see me. Like the wind and the clouds and the seabirds flying, I can never catch up.

2. A memory of school runs across snowy fields. I'm with Roger. We're the back-markers, left far behind. The track we're following is bare and stony. It climbs into sun then dips into shadow where no one can see us. Slowing to a walk, we pick our way over ice and frozen mud. Roger's face and legs are blotched red as if he's been drinking. I'm just ahead – *struggling on* as my father would say. I can hear him in my head, talking about war and the *fighting spirit*. For Roger and me it's not so easy. We're hot and cold and shivery. It's as if we're ill or being punished for something we haven't done. Although we don't know it, we're in the wilderness.

3. Another memory of Roger, this time sitting at a school desk. He's Roger-the-loon: a spindly boy with fidgety hands and chewed-down fingernails. He makes machine-type noises playing with his pen. His self-absorption seems like an act. He's me on a bad day.

4. A classroom scene with Roger and me. We've been told to study silently while the teacher *steps out*. The air is full of coughs and whispers and suppressed laughter. There's a note passing with a tree-and-hangman picture and our names underneath. When it reaches us we're supposed to laugh, but we don't. Instead Roger jumps up to throw it in the bin. Just as he deposits it, the teacher arrives. Loud exclamations follow, filling up the room. Suddenly I hear the smack-crack of a ruler on Roger's palm. I want to tell about the note, but can't. The words won't come.

5. I'm sitting by the window on the school bus. I can see my face in profile moving across houses and pavements. Although I know it's my reflection, I'm caught up in its expression as if it's a picture of someone else. The boy out there is an X-ray person who coasts through air. He has no shadow. As a version of me he's thin-skinned, all thought and images, and unreal. His wings float invisibly above the roughness of life. He's the ache I feel looking at the sky. He's everything I lack.

6. A picture from a family album of me at the chess-board, absorbed in calculation. I've one hand on my cheek and my gaze fixed on the centre of the board. I look as if I'm half-crazy. My adult opponent has his back to the camera. He's large and broad-shouldered and could be a policeman. I'm telling him my story. There's a line of investigation I want him to go down. He's looking for holes, testing my alibi. We're engaged in guerrilla warfare.

7. In my book, I'm walking alone through gorse and heather, forcing my own high. I have to feel everything –

the wind in my face, sunspots, pine scents and blue-lined hills – they're who I am. It's a dream-time walk with unreal voices and spirits watching. My friends, I call them. If I listen hard, I can hear them breathing.

In *The Dream of Great Writing* I'm super-alive. It's my sunlit upland with blue skies and lark song where I jump off on my own. In my mind I'm carrying a notebook to take things down. Every time I walk, I'm busy writing it …

In my imaginary library, I'm putting down a book, leaving it open in a chair. It's my dream catcher. I'm thinking back about how memory can grow and where I've got up to. Half-real, half made-up, it tells my story.

MOMENTS OF TRUTH

—— Leslie ——

So, at 69 I'm beginning to feel my age. And today's one of those days when I climb upstairs with both hands on the banisters. I don't know why my legs are so stiff, but it seems as if I need a push from behind. I've become two people: the frail old man moving with effort and the public me, taking painkillers and ignoring my legs. There's a third self who tries to believe that this isn't happening – but that's just wishful thinking. The fact is, I'm getting old.

When I reach the landing I pause. I imagine I'm a jogger taking a rest but ready to push on. I'm also rerunning breakfast with Sue, trying to make sense of my behaviour. Too often now I find myself complaining or overreacting to something. So if Sue talks politics I'm grouchy, or hurt. Part of me feels I'm letting her down, while another part wants to magically reverse everything that has happened – my darkness, her news-talk, and the mood that follows – because anything negative can set me off.

Of course I'm really too young to feel like this.

Upstairs, out of Sue's sight, I'm all fingers and thumbs. Simple tasks like fasteners or buttons are a fiddle, and I talk myself through them like a trainer. I'm not at my best and I soon reach my limit. It's as if I'm at the beginning of a game I've never played before. So, for example, computer problems are hard to put with, and when I can't find something in the wardrobe I get shaky and have to sit down. It takes what seems hours to get ready and leave the house, but I make myself to do it. As I say goodbye I kiss Sue and say sorry for my moods.

There's nothing wrong with my balance, but on the way to the shops my feet begin to drag and I stumble slightly. I'm aware that someone watching might think I've been drinking. In the supermarket I know what I want and for a moment it's as if I'm fourteen, untouched by age. But that soon changes. After I've paid I return, taking each step rhythmically, steadily, while pulling my trolley uphill. There's a strain in my legs and back, as if I'm carrying a brickie's hod. Somehow the earth's gravity has increased overnight. I don't fight against it but count as I walk, taking rests. Near the top I'm imagining a rope looped around my waist and I'm pulling myself up to the summit – where I meet another version of me, much younger and stronger, who doesn't feel the strain. I stay with that younger self for a while ...

The child in me believes I can do anything. If I can see something I imagine it's in my grasp, so I'll lift a heavy box or crouch down fixing a door, even though my back is complaining. Yes, there's a calculation involved, but maybe it's an unrealistic one. I know I need to exercise and extend my fitness – and I talk about a balance between caution and risk – but there is a real danger: I had a major back operation and to end in that level of pain again frightens me. But fear means nothing to my inner child. My child knows for sure nothing can touch her. When I walk with her, the sun's out and the street's an adventure. He/she doesn't feel their body, it's all part of the wind and light and the vehicles passing. Everything is out loud and new.

I hang on to that child-magic when I can. In company I forget my aches and pains and chat and smile with no sense of effort. When I meet people on the street or walk in the woods or visit gardens I'm in remission. Belief makes it possible to climb steep hills or carry heavy bags.

Of course, that kind of belief only works for a while. Like taking pills, its short-term effects can mask what the body's saying. So I have to be careful with myself. I'm lying in wait for the grumpy old person with the moods and stiffness and fingers fumbling on the climb upstairs.

I'm beginning to know myself.

—— *Sue* ——

The girl lost all her hair to alopecia and became a secret dolphin. Being adult didn't turn out as she had trusted. She blamed herself, and shrank. She was much better at pretending, and liked the disguise the wig gave her, but she was her biggest disappointment. Sometimes she couldn't forgive herself for the things she got wrong. When Daddy died, the grief was beyond imagining. And Mummy was braver than ever.

Then the woman met a beautiful boy. He wasn't really a boy and he preferred wearing dresses and flowery tops, but he was beautiful. The woman was thinner as well as older. She told him her biggest secrets, and the story of the little girl. She showed him her writing; he sent her his poems. He asked her to take off her wig and he didn't run away. He just loved her. And when she looked in the mirror she saw she'd changed inside.

This was a new kind of happiness, and she was afraid to lose it. The beautiful boy was sunny, funny, and brave. She loved his poems. They walked in gardens and kissed.

"You're beautiful," he said, stroking her bare head, "just the way you are."

"You can be totally honest," he said, "and fully yourself."

"You are strong enough to face the world without hiding," he told her, "and I will be proud to hold your hand."

So she never wore her wig again, didn't care what people did or said, and stopped hating mirrors.

He believed in her. So she became an author. She believed in him, and he did too. They were #AuthorsInLove and it was bruising, but thrilling. Soon she became ill, had procedures and operations and felt shame as well as pain. But he made her feel lovable anyway, and she owned her scars. The beautiful boy grew old too soon, and hurt all over, and lived with less sun and more night. She made him feel lovable anyway, and when he began to walk in the world in his dresses, she found it harder than she wanted to, but she was proud to hold his hand.

She began to work for change. For everything she had always believed was good and true. That meant peace, justice, and kindness, and one earth shared and cared for by all. She lived with despair in a world of war, refugees and climate breakdown, but doing what love required of her erased all fear.

Stories can't all end happily ever after. The best are about death as well as love. The path only leads in one direction, but they walked it together. And when the love was shaken or shadowed, they held on.

Inside the woman there was a girl who'd never stop being sorry, and sad. That was part of her story, but not all. And she wrote stories that made her cry because if they didn't, they were just pretend.

—— *Leslie* ——

So what would we be without our illnesses? Mine include glaucoma, an enlarged prostate, neck aches and leg cramps that wake me in the night, stomach pain, mouth sores, a calloused toe, thin skin that easily bruises, general fatigue, and stiffness/pain walking. They're a kind of second family – ever-present, difficult to predict and inclined to nag. Sometimes, because they're small, they gang up on me like an occupying force – one that keeps changing its angle of attack. More often they begin separately, overlap for a while, then lose interest or turn into something else. Some of them are what's called *run-ons*: hormonal processes that keep going and which I'd be better without; some are a kind of rust. They act as memento mori.

—— *Sue* ——

Back to the Future

"What happened to her hair?" asked Kate.

It was her first pastoral visit to the home and she'd expected sticks, frames, stoops and smells, even the odd Bertha Rochester laugh, but not a bald woman.

"Susie? She lost it all when she was young. We're trying to persuade her to wear a wig to keep warm."

Kate, who had started to sweat soon after entering the place, wondered whether the staff had a different motive. She didn't suppose elderly people were any kinder than children in the playground could be.

"Amazing earrings," she muttered, smiling at Susie and the large peace symbols stretching her ears to a point.

Susie smiled back.

"Used to be an activist," added the supervisor, whose name label said Tatiana. "Wrote books too. You haven't met her husband!"

Kate wasn't sure what that meant. Tatiana's phone sounded and she excused herself with the words, "Minor crisis."

Kate thought she should probably choose to sit next to someone with no partner in the Care Centre, a widow perhaps, but the chair next to Susie was empty. She was intrigued.

"Hello," she began. "I'm Kate, the new vicar of St John's, just round the corner. You're Susie?"

"Welcome, Kate." She smiled. "I was Sue until I came here. Sue on all the books. But I was Susie when I was small. It sounds young and playful so it helps me pretend!"

Kate noticed that she was dressed like a younger woman, in jeans and a baggy red jumper that didn't conceal how thin she was. With no hair to frame it, her face looked small, its dome surprising. Kate supposed all hidden scalps had their own individual shape and hoped she'd never discover hers, being rather attached to her thick, kinky hair for being unlikely in a priest. Conscious of its abundance now, she tucked some of it back behind her ear.

"I hear you were a writer?"

"Not a rich and famous one, thank goodness. I always loved making up stories. Writing them for less than a living was an enormous treat. When anyone used the L word about one of them I was beside myself with joy ..."

"L word?" Kate was thinking Lavatory because she'd noted it on the way in and wondered whether anyone under sixty would know what it meant.

"Love!" cried Susie. "My favourite word! Apart from passion, which is much the same."

"Ah, of course. Stupid of me." She asked Susie to name some of her titles and was told she didn't need to make out they meant anything to her. Which they didn't.

Susie ran one ridged hand over her scalp, forehead to neck, as if she was thinking hard – or just liked the way it felt. It wasn't wrinkled like the rest of her, but there were blue veins threading the white. Did she want to talk about it?

"I hear some people would like you to wear a wig," Kate ventured.

"I can't. They don't understand. It's not to cause offence. It was a stand I took, not to cover up just to fit in. To be myself. I didn't ask for the alopecia but it was nothing to be ashamed of. We can't all look like Helen of Troy." She grinned. "I would have said Julie Christie but I'd show my age!"

"That was brave," Kate told her.

"People said that a lot but it was the last thing I ever felt. It made me feel good, though, walking around with a bare head and being a bit ... funky, or edgy." She said the words with enjoyment, as if they were slightly naughty. "Women still get dictated to about how they look. It makes me mad."

"Me too," agreed Kate.

Susie didn't look angry. Rather, as she turned to the window onto the garden Kate thought unimaginative, she seemed sad.

"I wanted to change things. I came to it late, around the time I became a grandma, and there was so much to campaign for – and against. People prefer to believe in happy endings but you have to work for those." She leaned intently towards Kate. "Do you think we're making progress, enough? Will it be all right?"

Kate didn't know what to say because honestly, despair did no one any good. She was one of just four clergy in the town where there were once close to forty, and sometimes she thought all she was doing was trying to keep a grip on the past, when the future had to be completely different. *Thanks for trying anyway?*

"Sometimes, when I wasn't brave enough to live the activism myself, I wrote the story instead. We used to call that a cop out but stories are powerful. They can change lives. You should know that!"

Kate knew Quakers weren't big on literal interpretation of the Bible and she'd lost faith in that kind of religion herself, so took no offence.

"But I couldn't imagine this. Being old. How can you, when you're bendy and never run out of steam?"

Kate wasn't sure she was, or did, but she was glad to be mobile and free. Of course she was. No one wanted to end here.

"I have memories, and some of them are wonderful, but they're stories now. Maybe history's never as real as we think. Daddy made up stories and when we recognised something taken from the real world, ours, we bounced up and grinned from ear to ear, especially if our headmistress was stuck on the roof or upside down in a puddle!"

Kate laughed.

"Tell me about yourself or I'll babble on."

"Please do. I'm enjoying it."

"I hope you're loved, Kate – and not just by God."

Susie wanted to know about her children – really wanted to know, asked questions and squinted hard at the photos on Kate's phone.

"You like children," Kate observed.

"They're the easiest in the world to love because they still imagine. They don't draw that line between what's real and what's play, or there's a line but it's no firmer than a rubber band, and they have one foot on each side, like a skipping game. They live in worlds they've created so they have all the power but at the same time they're frightened because the dark is so full."

Kate winced thinking how much time her own kids spent on devices. She must do better.

"I know my death scares the young ones already." For the first time Susie looked sad. "They imagine it better than I can!"

"You're not afraid of death?"

Susie seemed to be considering. "I don't want to lose my proper self, the real me. Not that she was any great shakes. I've just about hung on to her but the body she's saddled with now needs a proper update. I've got six scars, you know."

Kate hoped she looked suitably sympathetic, but also that she wouldn't be shown.

"My insides are seriously dysfunctional and I always hated bad smells! I should apologise in advance. But I'm blessed, I know that. For one thing, I've still got my funny old stick! And here he comes!"

Looking to the door, Kate saw a tall, thin figure in a long cardigan with a twirly edge, an even longer flowery tunic and leggings that might be called magenta. Not a woman. His hair was white and feathery, and fell softly to his shoulders. Behind his glasses his eyes looked tired, raw-rimmed. He grimaced and breathed out sharply, but kept walking with the aid of his frame on wheels. Kate could see fine features behind his glasses. He'd been ... dashing, distinguished? But those might be the wrong words. Would he rather she said beautiful, once?

"Darling," Susie told him, "this is Kate."

"Nice to meet you."

"We shake this place up all right," he said.

His laugh was wild. Susie smiled. "Big imagination," she mouthed.

—— Cy ——

There are times I have been lucky to survive, both sober and drunk. I joined a specialist autistic school in Buckinghamshire and as a team-building exercise they sent us on an outward bound weekend to Wales. I didn't really want to be a teacher, but the comedy and acting weren't pulling in enough money. We spent the first evening in the pub, ending with drinking games and shots and then drinks back at the house until the early hours. In the morning I was woken up, still drunk, and told we were going mountain biking. So, with bleary eyes and numb fingers that had barely been able to tie up my own shoelaces, I found myself cycling with the group up painfully steep roads. After what seemed like hours of struggle we stopped and the instructor announced we had reached the starting point. The starting point?! Exchanging looks, I told him I thought I'd better go back. He agreed without too much persuasion. As I began to freewheel downhill with the open sky above and beautiful dense, emerald green walls on either side I felt free, like that small child riding my sister's blue tricycle. As I flew down the road and around the snakelike bends, the ecstatic part of my mind raised a warning finger and cleared its throat. "Ahem, this is a road. You're in the middle of it. What happens if something is driving up the hill?" Gripped by the voice, I pulled up and moved the bike over to the ditch. At that moment a huge truck burst round the bend, missing me by fractions of a second. My knees felt weak. I knew I had avoided The Angel of Death (to me forever embodied by a mermaid who visits me in my dreams) by a hair's breadth.

—— *Leslie* ——

I remember a counsellor telling me that the soul is at its peak when facing death. We grow towards the moment when we walk off stage. Watching a dear friend going through that process, I wrote this story in her voice ...

My Moment

My moment? There are so many, but now I've got you here, let me tell you about one, my biggest.

It begins in the front room. I'm spread across a mattress with my blister pack and post-its and letters of appointment. My side is playing up. It feels like wires in there, or a needle, digging for a vein. Stop it I say, I don't need you – shoo, vamoose, get lost. In my mind I'm swatting at wasps. But I tell myself to keep calm and begin by counting. Listen, I say, repeating numbers *1-2-3*, just hear those voices, *they* know what's best.

I remember back home jogging with a stitch, laughing in the sun. That hurt, too. I don't have the words, but I know the pain was different. Like sticking a toe in water – afterwards you can't feel how far it went in. Even then my body wasn't all there – not completely, not as I'd like it. I was the youngest, running here, running there. Every day the boys dared me, because I was a girl. And was I willing! You'd laugh if you saw me. Quick, quick, I said as I practised my getaways – on your marks, get set, go. When the Koevoet came I set off. Africa to London, like a hot animal, I ran.

The sweat comes in pools, soaking my head. I've fizzy by the bed and sweets in a bag. They're my big sticks, to whack away hypos. I'm a queen propped up on a pillow, and my land's out there. I can see the houses opposite and the birds in pairs – cheep-cheep – and the sun on roofs. When it's bad I count the tiles. One, two, three and four, I breathe don't think – dee dum dee dum – or take my own pulse. That one's a mossy one. It counts for two. And that one's broken. So four and a half, -ish. That keeps me busy. When it's not so bad I look at the windows and ask *who's in there?* Or stand at the door – *knock-knock, is anybody home?* It's like that game where's the church, where's the steeple? – open your hands and out come the people.

Houses are like minds. They can be all bricked up, or they can be light and glass. The people inside are closed in or they're wide open, like mouths. I've known a few – their names, their lives, their stories. Over the block, number 87 – that's Sandra's. Everyone knew her. When she was out and about, oh yes you could hear her coming. Her illnesses and ops, stories of the ward, the doctors she kissed. In the get-well group Sandra was the talker. She's not here now.

It's hot and I'm fat-cat-dreamy. I see bodies on Henman Hill. It's a record-breaking final. I'm out in the sun running. 5 – 2 down, playing for life. I'm getting it back, baselining. It's love-forty, second serve, but I'm still standing. I'm here, my name's on the scoreboard, and my T-shirt says NEVER EVER EVER EVER EVER GIVE UP ...

That's one moment. Not *the* moment, but a run-through. How it ends, I don't know. Maybe I fall asleep or the phone rings or it's time for my pills – whatever it is I get through, and pop back up like a flower after rain.

I'm lucky, my friends keep me going. They turn up everywhere, out of the blue. When I'm alone I imagine them here, gathered around. It's like that film I once saw of people on a beach. When one person's dancing no one looks, but when someone joins in then everyone's soon up, doing the conga. My friends are like that. They're the callers on the phone, the writers and texters, the helpers and visitors and bedside well-wishers – and I say to them, oh, you're all in my heart. But most of all and top of my list, Hannah and Andrew. They're my best angels. They know me well.

When they're coming, I'm a bit shaky. It's party time. I'm embarrassed as well. The flat's a mess and the come-in helpers aren't much good. But when I call Hannah and Andrew, they won't be stopped. And when they arrive it seems like they've always been there. "Make yourself at home, kids," I say, as if they were my lovey-doveys, my teeny-weenies. They laugh because they're sixty like me, and say it's just the right age. It is, for them.

Hannah's so soft-centred. Her hand squeezes mine and we smile.

"How've you been, Annie?" she asks and I answer quietly, telling my story. I find myself long-faced, speaking seriously, like someone on camera. The words are mine but strange. They keep me together.

When Andrew comes in, I'm talking about hospital. He sits and listens, touching Hannah's hand. When I've talked myself out, he makes a joke. It's one of those upside-down, topsy-turvy, truly, madly jokes that I enjoy. About me propping up the service, keeping the medics in a job. We all laugh, and he talks about doctors as servants and my holidays in hospital. Then he's adding up the wards I've been in, calling it My Royal Tour. And now I'm seeing something, a scene up ahead. It's another of those pictures, like the view out of the window and the child on the run, and he's in it ...

My second big moment is on the stairs. Andrew's by my side, talking gently. I'm crouched hurting. I'm an animal, and I've been run over. I've slipped, like a climber, and my body's broken. I'm looking down on myself from the white walls above. It's what I call my afterlife dream. One of those horrible all-night aches, stronger than morphine or shouting. And the stairs are where I've ended. His voice is by me – or is it inside? – telling me he's with me. Then I'm in twilight. It's a desert island; the sea's coming in ...

When the third moment comes, I'm somewhere else. Look, I think, who's that woman? She's coughing like a crow. In a way, she's turned inside out. Maybe taking wings. Yes, I can see her, the crow woman's being lifted. And now the air's turning grey and the windows are steaming up. But the room's still here, holding me down, and I can hear people praying. Hannah and Andrew, I think.

Does my life pass before me? I'm not quite sure. I'm in it somewhere, here and now *and* at a distance. Then it's all happened – all the blood and the mess and the tubes and drips and pills in cups – and now it's the dream of being dreamed. By someone, by anyone, I don't know who.

And, if it's come to this, how can I can describe it? Nothing prepared me.

I've been through my story and out the other side. I'm close to that other place where nothing is real. My body's empty. My life, what was that? It detaches and detaches, and now it's gone. Even Hannah and Andrew.

And this is my moment.

Photos

p6   Leslie.
p10 "Little Sue" sitting on the stone.
p13 A young Sam and Cy.
P14 "Escape" by Cy Henty.
p23 Sue as Little John.
p28 "Little Sue" in a kilt.
p31 Leslie playing chess.
p34 Sam and Cy's show for their 40th birthdays. Photographed by Dan Maher, poster artwork by Dan Butler.
p38 Leslie's Grandfather in The Mikado.
p42 *Heaven's Rage* Alcohol Scene, photo by Mark Crane.
p44 Cy Henty as Rosebrook in Pat Higgins' film *Killer Killer*. Photograph by Debbie Attwell.
p47 Sparkle the lion troll, photo by Sheelagh Frew Crane.
p52 Artwork by Cy Henty based on the characters from Al Ronald's film *Harriet's war*.
p54 My Crazy Hand poster, artwork by Molly Brown.
p56 Leslie being filmed for the Genderhouse Festival, photo by Dagmara Bilon.
p63 "Little Sue" on the beach.
p76 Cy's alter ego escaping through the looking glass.
p77 Cy Henty as Snod in *The Butterfly Effect*.
p79 Leslie in the back garden.
p95 Sue with bicycle 1967
p97 Sam and Cy performing as newlyweds "Trevor and Sheila" at The King's Head Theatre, their first full London show.
p109 Sue with birthday typewriter 1972.
p112 Leslie Tate outdoors, photo by Gemma Driver.
p121 Leslie Tate indoors, photo by Gemma Driver.
p128 "Asylum" by Cy Henty.
p137 Sue at home 1978.
p158 Sue and Leslie walking in Dockey Wood, photo by Gwynneth Shiers.
p175 An original Electric Head poster. Photography by Debbie Attwell, artwork by Al Ronald.
p176 Al Ronald and Cy Henty rehearsing for their St Peter and the Viking Sketch, photography Debbie Attwell.

p180   Concept artwork for The Electric Heads' film, *Wrong Way Round*.

p181   Cy Henty as Mr Scrote for The Electric Head Pilot, *The Cracks Are Showing*.

p188   Activist Sue.

p204   Leslie reading at a Milton Keynes Foodbank Event, photo by Ashra Burnham.

p209   "Tie" by Cy Henty.

p211   Caricature of Bern by Cy Henty.

p215   Leslie, photo by Sheelagh Frew Crane.

p225   Angel of Death by Cy Henty with fractal artwork by Tom Milner.

www.ingramcontent.com/pod-product-compliance
Lightning Source LLC
Chambersburg PA
CBHW071712160426
43195CB00012B/1660